# AROUND BRITAIN

## D*a*IRY COOKBOOK

| | |
|---|---|
| Executive Editor | Nick Rowe |
| Managing Editor | Emily Anderson |
| Editor | Emma Callery |
| Designer | Karen Raison |
| Regional guides text | Sean Callery |
| Proofreader | Kathie Gill |
| Indexer | Hilary Bird |
| | |
| Food Photographer | Steve Lee |
| Food Stylist | Sara Lewis |
| Props Stylist | Jo Harris |
| | |
| Recipes created by | Pat Alburey |
| | Kathryn Hawkins |
| | Sue McMahon |
| | Kate Moseley |
| | |
| Research Dietitian | Dr Wendy Doyle |
| | |
| Recipe testers | Iain Anderson |
| | Angela Broad |
| | Sarah Broad |
| | Helen Cookson |
| | Carolyn Glazebrook |
| | Katy Johnson |
| | Natalie Meadowcroft |
| | Anne-Marie Neild |
| | Pam Shore |
| | Peter Tantram |
| | |
| Flower Photographer | Nikki English |
| | |
| Production | Mo Adams |
| | Priti Kothary |

Eaglemoss Consumer Publications Ltd
Electra House, Electra Way,
Crewe, Cheshire, CW1 6WZ
Telephone 01270 270050
Website www.dairydiary.co.uk

First printed March 2006

© Eaglemoss Consumer Publications Ltd

Picture credits: Alamy (Peter Adams) 155, (Adams Picture Library t/a apl) 8, (Rob Bartee) 111, (Mark Bauer) 163, (Cephas Picture Library) 10, 155, (Richard Cooke) 16, (Elmtree Images) 14, 75, (Robert Estall photo agency) 107, (Foodfolio) 75, (Ian Francis) 22, (Jason Friend) 127, (Leslie Garland Picture Library) 137, 145, 177, (Carole Hallett) 168, 171, (Robert Harding Picture Library) 45, 131, 151, (Jeremy Hoare) 137, (Andrew Holt) 151, (Doug Houghton) 29, (ImageState) 75, 81, (Mike Kipling) 11, 145, 177, (Nigel Lloyd) 18, (David Lyons) 17, 87, 111, (Louisa Macdonell) 29, (John Martin) 45, (Medioimages) 5, 19, 137, (David Noble) 5, 9, 87, (David Noton) 13, 127, 163, (Photofusion Picture Library) 81, (Les Polders) 107, (Popperfoto) 12, (Rob Rayworth) 23, 95, (The National Trust Photolibrary) 21, 65, (The Photolibrary Wales) 95, (Worldwide Picture Library) 15, 131; Eaglemoss (Karl Adamson) 87, 163, 177, (Edward Allwright) 131, (Emily Anderson), (Nikki English) 8-192(flower shots), (Food Features) 163, (Ian Garlick) 29, (Matthew Griffiths) 45, 81, 145, 155, (Joff Lee) 151, (Steve Lee) 1-192(recipes shots), (Northern Counties) 65, 127, (Simon Smith) 111, (Frank Weider) 95, 107; Getty Images (Joe Cornish) cover.

Poetry list: p64 extract from 'Teignmouth' by John Keats (1795–1821); p74 extract from a letter by Susanna Blamire (1747–1794); p80 extract from 'Song' by William Blake (1757–1827); p86 extract from 'The Highlands Swelling Blue' Lord Byron (1788–1824); p94 extract from 'Hunting Song' by Samuel Taylor Coleridge (1772–1834); p126 extract from 'The Passionate Shepherd to His Love' by Christopher Marlowe (1543–1607); p154 extract from 'Here's to You Again' by Alexander Rodger (1784–1846); p162 extract from 'To Clotted Cream' by Edward Capern (1819–1894).

# Contents

# Introduction and cook's information

For a small nation, the topography of Britain is immensely varied. This fertile land yields the ingredients that have influenced our gastronomic heritage. From the orchards of the South East to the lochs of Scotland, each region harvests its own food and creates its own dishes. Some recipes in this book have evolved over decades, others are brand new. All have been written for today's cook, using simple techniques and readily available ingredients.

## Dry weight conversions

| Recommended grams (g) | Imperial ounces (oz) |
|---|---|
| 15 | ½ |
| 25 | 1 |
| 50 | 2 |
| 75 | 3 |
| 110 | 4 (¼lb) |
| 150 | 5 |
| 175 | 6 |
| 200 | 7 |
| 225 | 8 (½lb) |
| 250 | 9 |
| 275 | 10 |
| 300 | 11 |
| 350 | 12 (¾lb) |
| 375 | 13 |
| 400 | 14 |
| 425 | 15 |
| 450 | 16 (1lb) |
| 500 | 1lb 2oz |
| 680 | 1½lb |
| 750 | 1lb 10oz |
| 900 | 2lb |

These quantities are not exact, but they have been calculated to give proportionately correct measurements.

## Spoon measures

| | |
|---|---|
| 1 tablespoon | = 3 level teaspoons |
| 1 level tablespoon | = 15ml |
| 1 level teaspoon | = 5ml |

If greater accuracy is not required:

| | |
|---|---|
| 1 rounded teaspoon | = 2 level teaspoons |
| 1 heaped teaspoon | = 3 level teaspoons or 1 level tablespoon |

## Liquid conversions

| Metric (ml) | Imperial (fl oz) | US cups |
|---|---|---|
| 15 | ½ | 1 tbsp (level) |
| 30 | 1 | ⅛ |
| 60 | 2 | ¼ |
| 90 | 3 | ⅜ |
| 125 | 4 | ½ |
| 150 | 5 (¼ pint) | ⅔ |
| 175 | 6 | ¾ |
| 225 | 8 | 1 |
| 300 | 10 (½ pint) | 1¼ |
| 350 | 12 | 1½ |
| 450 | 16 | 2 |
| 500 | 18 | 2¼ |
| 600 | 20 (1 pint) | 2½ |
| 900 | 1½ pints | 3¾ |
| 1 litre | 1¾ pints | 1 quart (4 cups) |
| 1.25 litres | 2 pints | 1¼ quarts |
| 1.5 litres | 2½ pints | 3 US pints |
| 2 litres | 3½ pints | 2 quarts |

| | | |
|---|---|---|
| 568ml = 1 UK pint | (20fl oz) | 16fl oz = 1 US pint |

These quantities are not exact, but they have been calculated to give proportionately correct measurements.

## Estimated average requirements

Estimated average requirements (EARs) are the amount of nutrients or energy required each day for the average adult.

| | Calories | Saturated fat | Salt | Fibre |
|---|---|---|---|---|
| Women | 1900 | 11g | less than 6g | 18g |
| Men | 2550 | 11g | less than 6g | 18g |

## Oven temperatures

| °C | °F | Gas mark | Description |
|---|---|---|---|
| 110 | 225 | ¼ | cool |
| 120/130 | 250 | ½ | cool |
| 140 | 275 | 1 | very low |
| 150 | 300 | 2 | very low |
| 160/170 | 325 | 3 | low to moderate |
| 180 | 350 | 4 | moderate |
| 190 | 375 | 5 | moderately hot |
| 200 | 400 | 6 | hot |
| 220 | 425 | 7 | hot |
| 230 | 450 | 8 | hot |
| 240 | 475 | 9 | very hot |

Guide to recommended equivalent settings, not exact conversions. Always refer to your cooker instruction book.

## Grilling times: fish

| Type of fish | Grilling time |
|---|---|
| Cod (steak) | 5–6 min each side |
| Dover sole (whole) | 4–6 min each side |
| Dover sole (fillet) | 2–3 min each side |
| Halibut (steak) | 5–6 min each side |
| Herring (whole) | 4–5 min each side |
| Mackerel (whole) | 6–7 min each side |
| Monkfish (steak) | 5–6 min each side |
| Plaice (whole) | 4–6 min each side |
| Plaice (fillet) | 2–3 min each side |
| Salmon (steak) | 5–6 min each side |
| Tuna (steak) | 1–2 min each side |

Times given for fish weighing approximately 175–225g (6–8 oz).

## Roasting times: meat

Set oven temperature to 180°C/350°F/Gas 4.

| | Cooking time per 450g/1lb | Extra cooking time |
|---|---|---|
| **Beef** | | |
| Rare | 20 min | 20 min |
| Medium | 25 min | 25 min |
| Well done | 30 min | 30 min |
| **Lamb** | | |
| Medium | 25 min | 25 min |
| Well done | 30 min | 30 min |
| **Pork** | | |
| Medium | 30 min | 30 min |
| Well done | 35 min | 35 min |

Let the cooked meat rest for 5–15 minutes before carving to allow the juices to be reabsorbed and to make carving easier.

## Steaming times: vegetables

| Vegetable | Steaming time |
|---|---|
| Asparagus | 5–7 min |
| Beansprouts | 3–4 min |
| Beetroot (sliced) | 5–7 min |
| Broccoli (florets) | 5–7 min |
| Brussels sprouts | 5–7 min |
| Cabbage (chopped) | 4–6 min |
| Cauliflower (florets) | 5–7 min |
| Carrots (thickly sliced) | 5–7 min |
| Courgettes (sliced) | 3–5 min |
| Green beans | 5–7 min |
| Leeks | 5–8 min |
| Mangetout peas | 3–5 min |
| Peas | 3–5 min |
| Potatoes (cubed) | 5–7 min |

Times given are for steaming from when water has started to boil.

## Roasting times: poultry

| | Oven temperature | Cooking time per 450g/1lb | Extra cooking time | Resting time |
|---|---|---|---|---|
| Chicken | 200°C/400°F/Gas 6 | 20 min | 30 min | 15 min |
| **Turkey (stuffed weight)** | | | | |
| small (under 6kg/13lb) | 200°C/400°F/Gas 6 | 12 min | 20 min | 30 min |
| large | 180°C/350°F/Gas 4 | 16 min | – | 30 min |
| Duck | 200°C/400°F/Gas 6 for 45 min then 180°C/350°F/Gas 4 | 35 min | – | 15 min |

# Scotland

Scotland is a country with many contrasts. Life in the lush meadowlands of the southern Borders has always been different from that on the harsh bare hills of the Grampians in the north, or from that on the fiercely independent islands scattered in the cold, grey North Sea.

With so many islands and its ragged coastline, the sea has long provided food for the Scottish diet. The busy ports of Peterhead and Aberdeen continue to unload large catches of herring, haddock, mackerel, halibut, sole and cod, while salmon and trout are still caught wild but also reared in giant fish farms in fresh or seawater lochs. Lobster and shrimp are caught off the Borders coast, while the Western Isles also supply scallops and winkles.

Long hours working outside in the cold and wet instilled a need for filling, hearty fare, best illustrated by the Scottish love of breakfast porridge: nutritious enough to satisfy the appetite until lunchtime, and usually flavoured with salt (though honey is not frowned upon). Similarly comforting are Scottish soups such as Scotch broth (mutton and pearl barley), cock-a-leekie (boiled fowl) (page 31) and cullen skink (Finnan haddock with potato) (page 28).

Oats have long been a mainstay of the Scottish diet, good for thickening stews and soups and grown because the crop can withstand poor soil and harsh weather. However, the milder climate and more fertile ground elsewhere enable Scotland to produce vast quantities of soft fruits, such as raspberries and strawberries. The sweet and the savoury unite in the Scottish love for baking a huge variety of cakes and biscuits, famous examples including the almond-topped Dundee cake (page 90), the rich, black bun fruit cake, bannocks (oat and barley biscuits cooked on the griddle), and melt-in-the-mouth buttery shortbread (page 73).

The Scottish moors and mountains also provide a wide selection of meat: sheep thrive on the rough slopes, and Scottish beef fed on the lush lowland grass is renowned the world over. An abundance of game inhabits the moors and forests, with deer (venison), grouse, partridge and pheasant being the best known. Perhaps the most famous Scottish meat dish is the haggis, the boiled and minced insides of a sheep mixed with beef suet and oatmeal then boiled or baked in the bag of the sheep's stomach (page 174). It tastes a lot better than it sounds!

## Ben Nevis, Burns and Balmoral

If you enjoy mountain walking, poetry or royalty spotting then at least one of this trio will appeal to you. At 1343m (4406ft), Ben Nevis is Britain's highest mountain, its impact increased by its setting on the shore line of Loch Linnhe above the town of Fort William. The Gaelic name has links with words meaning poisonous or terrible, perhaps fitting in that it is known for weather changes that can catch out unwary walkers and climbers.

Robert Burns is the best-loved Scottish poet, because of the enduring quality of his writing and his high-spirited character. He wrote well-known songs such as 'Auld Lang Syne' and 'My Love is Like a Red Red Rose', but is also famous for his use of humour and dialect in writing about the lives of his fellow rural Scots. Two such masterpieces are 'Tam O'Shanter' and 'The Jolly Beggars'.

Finally, we come to the estate and castle of Balmoral, built around 1854 for Prince Albert and Queen Victoria, who described it in her journals as 'my dear paradise in the Highlands'. The finest of many castles in scenic Royal Deeside, it is the private home of the Royal family, who spend two months in it each autumn. The estate, most of which is accessible to the public, covers more than 50,000 acres of woodland and heather-clad hills.

**Above: Haggis, neeps and tatties (page 174) and, right, Dundee cake (page 90).**

Dairy farming has long flourished throughout Scotland, and recently cheese making has been revitalised with the manufacture of a wide range of traditional and contemporary home-produced cheeses in addition to the popular Scottish Cheddar.

Although one-pot cooking and smoke-cured meat and fish (such as the Arbroath Smokie) is part of the Scottish heritage, there is also a long tradition of fine eating. Steaks are served with sauces made with rare malt whiskies, and many cooking terms have survived from the days of the French alliance hundreds of years ago. Scottish cuisine is varied in its ingredients, flavours and influences.

INTRODUCTION

# North East and Yorkshire

Northumberland's wild and beautiful landscape boasts a dramatic untamed coastline, craggy hills and low-lying plains. A network of rivers weaves through the North East on to Yorkshire's desolate moors and the famous dales.

The sea has long provided much of the region's food, for example, kippers have been smoked over oak fires in the pretty harbour of Craster for more than 100 years.

Other regional fare includes the potato and cheese supper of pan haggerty (see page 36), one of several recipes that combine vegetables with cheese – which is itself made in numerous dairies across the region.

Scones and griddle cakes such as singin' hinnies (pages 58 and 67) are particularly popular in the region, as is the steamed, lemon-flavoured Newcastle pudding. However, a top favourite is the stottie cake, which isn't a cake at all: it's a savoury bread that is great for bacon or chip butties.

Another traditional Northumbrian dish is pease pudding, made using split peas, usually served with pork. Indeed, this meat is probably the best loved in both this region and Yorkshire to the south, where the delicate pink and mild flavour of York ham comes from the dry-salt curing method, which has been exported around the globe. Yorkshire's countryside features bleak moors, verdant dales and sweeping valleys as well as the industrial cities of Leeds and Bradford and the historic centre of York.

Sheep flourish in the gritty, bleak moors landscape and their milk was made into cheese before it was replaced by milk from the cows who populated the grassy lowlands. It is made into cheese such as tangy, crumbly Wensleydale (traditionally accompanied by apple pie), and is an ingredient in Yorkshire curd tart, an early version of cheesecake.

The Yorkshire palate seems to appreciate particularly dark, rich, sweet goods such as the classic comfort food parkin, a moist, heavy gingerbread made with oatmeal and black treacle, which used to be put in to cook as the bread oven cooled. It can often be found alongside buttered toasted teacakes and the wonderfully named old peculiar cake in the many excellent teashops that flourish in Yorkshire.

However, the dish many people think of when the county is mentioned in relation to food is

## The Dales, Durham and Hadrian's Wall

Three magnificent settings in this region are linked by one key component: rock. Starting with it in natural form, in the Yorkshire Dales limestone has eroded to leave lush valleys ('dales') crested by white limestone cliffs, known as 'scars'. Towering over both are the millstone grit cliffs known as 'fells'. The result is stunning and varied scenery where the criss-crossing stone walls built to stop the sheep straying seem as much part of the landscape as the huge waterfalls and the ridge of the Pennine Way.

To the north, yellow sandstone is the material from which one of the high points of cathedral architecture was created. Much of Durham Cathedral dates back some 900 years, and three main innovations of the revolutionary Gothic style come together in this building with its pointed arches, ribbed vaults and flying buttresses

North again, and back in time, we find another extraordinary engineering project: Hadrian's Wall, the famous barrier to stop northern tribes rampaging into the Roman-controlled land to the south. Built nearly 2000 years ago, the wall stretches 55 miles from west of Carlisle to the mouth of the River Tyne on the east coast, and was wide enough in places for soldiers to march three abreast. Parts of the wall still survive, and Housesteads in Northumberland is the location of the best preserved of its 13 army posts.

Left: Toad in the hole (page 120) and, above, Knickerbocker glory (page 144).

Yorkshire pudding (page 180), a batter of plain flour, eggs and milk or milk and water that was once cooked on an open fire underneath the roasting meat so that it soaked up the dripping juices. True Yorkshire hosts serve their 'puddings' as an appetite-quenching first course, rather than with the meat.

Any summary of Yorkshire fare would be incomplete without crediting the county with the finest fish and chips in the land, where the abundant produce of the North Sea is served in crisp batter with mushy peas and chips given extra flavour by being fried in lard. That said, today, the influence of Asian cooking is strong in towns such as Bradford, where folk are more likely to participate in an authentically prepared curry than paper-wrapped fish and chips.

# North West

The North West includes the Lake District, Cheshire and Lancashire, taking in the great cities of Liverpool and Manchester. From the tarns of Cumbria to the grassy plains of Cheshire there is a wealth of fantastic scenery and superb food.

Most of the traditional dishes are clearly developed to be suitable for feeding hard-working people who have to cope with a bracing climate. Many meat dishes would be made with lamb because so many sheep graze on the hills of this region. A typically robust meal would be Lancashire hot pot, a lamb stew incorporating the potatoes and other root vegetables grown so widely in the area.

Similarly appealing to the thrifty is tripe, which is a cow's stomach lining, usually served with onions, and black pudding, an earthy dish made from blood and oatmeal with many variations, all claiming to be the

best. The famous long Cumberland sausage is another dish that uses the less appealing parts of an animal so that nothing is wasted.

The sea, lakes and rivers provide more delicate flavours, such as the shrimps of Morecambe Bay (page 40) and stuffed herring and trout, which are caught on the line and increasingly farmed in the region. A real local speciality is the mild-flavoured char (page 105), a relative of the salmon, which got left behind in the Lakes after the Ice Age.

This region also boasts two of the finest British cheeses: Cheshire and Lancashire. White, crumbly Cheshire is mentioned

in the eleventh-century Domesday Book and was the only cheese that the British Navy would stock on board in the eighteenth century. Lancashire is creamier and is regarded as one of the best cooking and, especially, toasting cheeses as it melts into a velvety mass when heated. If you're fond of a cheese sandwich, large wholemeal flour bread rolls, or baps, are popular in the region, being an ideal way to eat in a hurry. They are also known as 'barm cakes' after a Lancashire word for the froth on liquid that contains yeast.

Similarly long on history are Eccles cakes, small, flat, raisin-filled pastries, which date from

## The Lakes, Lowry and Liverpool

The North West has inspired some of England's best-known poetry, painting and music. The postcard-perfect mountains and tarns of the Lake District attract walkers and lovers of beautiful scenery from around the world. The landscape is fundamental to the romantic poetry of William Wordsworth, who lived here for over eight years. It was also later home to Beatrix Potter, author and illustrator of the charming children's stories that introduced us to Peter Rabbit and his friends.

By way of contrast, the industrial landscape of Manchester with its smoking towers forming the horizon was the setting for many paintings

by L. S. Lowry. Lowry lived and worked as a rent collector and cashier in Salford, using his spare time to paint scenes of local life populated by his distinctive 'matchstick men' in drab urban colours. Although he painted in other styles, too, it was these pictures that eventually earned him fame towards the end of his life before he died in 1976.

By then The Beatles had also made their contribution to popular culture with a huge catalogue of music that is still much loved. The extraordinarily varied songs of John Lennon and Paul McCartney, combined with the experimental

leanings of guitarist George Harrison and the rock-solid drumming of Ringo Starr, reflected the changing lives of four Merseyside 'mop tops' who became the world's greatest pop stars in the 1960s and led the way in innovating new ways to write and record music.

at least the eighteenth century. They are closely related to the larger but equally convenient sweet, hand-held and fruity Chorley cake. Another great Northern comfort food is gingerbread, closely identified with the Lake District village of Grasmere. It is usually a crisp spicy biscuit and therefore offers a contrasting texture to the more moist parkin cake that originates across the Pennines in Yorkshire.

Simnel cake (page 178) is now closely identified with Easter, but one early version of it was known as Bury simnel cake at a time when it was traditionally a gift taken by serving girls returning home on Mothering Sunday. Its link with Easter probably stems from the 11 pieces of marzipan used to decorate its top – one for each true disciple.

**Above: Morecambe Bay potted shrimps (page 40); above right: roast lamb with apricots (page 126) and, right, Simnel cake (page 178).**

Finally, have you ever wondered where the Liverpool term 'scouser' comes from? It seems to be from a popular Merseyside dish rather like Irish stew, which was similar to a Scandinavian dish known as lobscaus. The stew became known as 'scouse', and use of the name broadened to mean a local person.

INTRODUCTION

# Western England

The shire counties are sometimes known as the Heart of England and certainly the rolling Malvern Hills, the honey-stone Cotswold cottages and the orchards seen in these western regions are quintessentially English sights.

The region is a foody's delight for every year the Ludlow Food Fair highlights the huge variety of excellent fare on offer. The warm, moist climate and rich, heavy soil create fertile conditions for fruit and vegetables, while the grassy hills have long been populated by sheep, which provide meat and wool for the weaving industries.

But it is dairy farming in this region that provides ingredients for its well-known chocolate bars and yogurt desserts. Also renowned for cheeses, such as the golden Double Gloucester, excellent in a variation of Welsh rarebit called Gloucester cheese and ale (page 34), where cheese and mustard are baked in brown ale. Land where cows graze

happily will also fatten beef cattle and this region hosts the famous white-faced Hereford breed, which produces meat of great flavour and tenderness. The sheep that graze the Cotswold Hills have inspired many lamb dishes, including the curiously named Gloucestershire squab pie, which blends the meat with spices and apple, and the equally misleading Oxford John steak (page 124), which is actually leg of lamb with capers. Other popular meat dishes in this region are faggots (originally made from liver in a thick sauce known as caul) and the beef-based Warwickshire stew. However, pork is the meat mainstay, perhaps because pigs once did the job of removing the windfalls in the apple, pear and plum orchards of this region. There is even a 'Midlands cut' of bacon, and a dish popular on the borders of the Welsh Marches is loin of pork with cabbage cake.

While we're on the subject of cake, there are several notable recipes from Western England. Brandy snaps (see page 71) and gingerbread are both local favourites. Staffordshire fruit cake is a well-known recipe made extra rich with the addition of black treacle and brandy; there is also a spiced Oxford cake and, best known of all, the Banbury cakes originating from that north Oxfordshire town. These are

## Castles, Cotswolds and Crockery

Western England provides a miniature history of Britain. It starts with the infighting between different regions and the quest for the English crown, which led to the building of huge fortresses to protect land and power. The best preserved example of a medieval castle in Britain is at Warwick, where the immense proportions of this 1000-year-old fortress are still a formidable sight. Less intact but full of history is Ludlow Castle, home to Princes Edward and Richard, the sons of Edward IV who were taken to the Tower of London and most probably murdered there. Another fine ruin is Kenilworth, immortalised by Sir Walter Scott in his nineteenth-century novel of the same name.

In medieval Britain the unlikely powerbase of the economy was the Cotswolds because this sheep-rearing region produced the wool vital for clothing and trade. Numerous homes and churches were built in the local honey-

coloured limestone and today these form the 'chocolate box' landscape of middle England.

The decline of the wool trade (which, ironically, helped to preserve this landscape) reflected a change to an industrial economy epitomised by the Potteries in Staffordshire. Abundant local supplies of the raw material clay, salt and lead for glazing and coal for firing kilns, led firms such as Wedgwood, Royal Doulton and Spode to manufacture their earthenware and stoneware here. It wasn't pretty, but it created the English ceramic industry.

made from puff pastry filled with raisins and dried fruits. Other eponymous recipes include Shrewsbury biscuits (page 77), which are rather like shortbread, Coventry God cakes (a traditional christening gift from godparents) and the great favourite of Staffordshire, oat cakes, which are closer to pancakes than oat biscuits and can be eaten with sweet or savoury accompaniments.

No review of the food from this area can omit mentioning the famous Worcestershire Sauce, a liquid that adds flavour to almost any savoury recipe and which originated when the Governor of Bengal returned to his native Worcester and tried to re-create an Indian recipe. The sauce was a complete disaster until tasted after several months when it had matured into the fine ingredient still used today.

**Above left: Gloucester cheese and ale (page 34); centre: Painswick bacon chops (page 119) and, above, brandy snaps (page 71).**

Similarly bizarre is the heritage of Cooper's Oxford marmalade, which is famous for its chunks of bitter peel from a variety of Seville oranges grown in Andalusia. Apparently, hardly anybody else can use the fruit because it's so bitter!

# Eastern England

Go east across England and the landscape becomes flatter as the horizon slips into the distance. This is a land of wide spaces and cinematic skies and is home to the arable farmlands of Britain. The climate is perfect for a wide range of crops and animal rearing.

INTRODUCTION

Our journey starts in the east Midlands counties of Derbyshire and Leicestershire, where high levels of dairy farming have stimulated the development of great cheeses such as flaky, tangy Red Leicester, green-tinged Sage Derby and creamy Stilton. This last takes its name from the village where an innkeeper first served the open-textured cheese to visitors, although, in fact, it was apparently made by his brother-in-law miles away in Melton Mowbray. This 'King of Cheeses' is delicious on its own, but can be used also in hot or cold recipes.

Wander on eastwards and we reach the fertile, wide fields of Lincolnshire where early vegetables and crisp celery burst from the soil. We can range through more vegetable fields as we travel south and pause to admire the gooseberries and gages (delicious in fruit tarts) of Cambridgeshire. This fertile region, sometimes called 'the food basket of Britain' produces cereals, flowers, fruits and vegetables. Notable recipes include celery baked in cream, the bacon and apple-filled fidget pie (page 121), and Trinity College pudding (page 150), an early version of the Christmas pudding.

The land is noticeably flatter as we head across the reclaimed fertile earth of the Fens to the Norfolk Broads. The mild climate stimulates farming of soft fruits such as strawberries, redcurrants, raspberries and blackcurrants, which create the wonderful deep

reds and tender pinks of a summer pudding.

Here rabbit stew and jugged hare were once popular choices for those who could not afford beef and lamb. Nowadays, though, Norfolk is famed for its huge production of turkeys, including the famous Norfolk Blacks. However, the fields of wheat, barley and rye and the flat

## The Peaks, the Broads and the Red Arrows

Eastern England is home to three contrasting scenes: an extraordinary natural landscape, another that was created by man hundreds of years ago, and one

sight which is completely man-made but no less compelling.

The Peak District is a wild area of deep-cut limestone dales with fast-flowing rivers and gorges and bleak high moors that remind us how uncompromising parts of our landscape can be. This land is wonderful for walking in but also attracts climbers, hang-gliders, cavers, pot-holers and fishermen.

Across to the east, the Norfolk Broads is another magnet for visitors, especially those who love boating. Peat harvesting during the Middle Ages led to floods that created broad, shallow lakes lying along five major rivers. It provides a habitat for many rare plant and animal species and a multitude of birds.

Not far away from the Norfolk Broads in Lincolnshire is the home of one of the world's premier aerobatic teams, the Red Arrows. The public face of the Royal Air Force, the Red Arrows demonstrate their professional excellence, thrilling crowds with the precision and intricacy of their aerobatic displays, including their trademark diamond nine formation.

Left: Greengage tart (page 161) and, right, Huntingdon fidget pie (page 121).

fens host many game birds such as partridge, quail and woodcock.

One notable Norfolk speciality is samphire, a juicy marsh plant sold all across the area. When boiled or blanched it tastes like slightly salty asparagus. This, of course, brings us to a more widely enjoyed seasonal crop: asparagus, served with hollandaise or white cheese sauce.

In days gone by, the port of Great Yarmouth would become so full of fishing boats unloading herring that it was said you could walk across the harbour just by stepping from deck to deck. The boats are gone but the smokehouses now cure red herrings and bloaters, mainly for export. However, grilled Norfolk herrings can be matched with another local crop, the yellow English mustard grown around Norwich, for a zingily spicy meal.

All along this Eastern coast are villages specialising in harvesting the sea for some of its produce, such as cockles and whelks. The best example is Cromer, where the dark meat of the small but succulent crabs is considered a great delicacy as used in recipes such as baked Cromer crab.

# South East

The South East of England benefits from a warm, moist climate and fertile soil, allowing its farmers to grow and raise almost anything, which is just as well, because the ever-expanding capital city of London has an enormous appetite.

INTRODUCTION

The lush green county of Kent has long been known as 'The Garden of England', and the rolling hills of Sussex and the plains of Hampshire are farmed extensively too. All of these counties border onto the English Channel, which is a valuable source of an enormous variety of fish and shellfish.

Many varieties of apples, pears, plums, cherries (introduced by the Romans) and soft fruits have been cultivated in Kent since at least Tudor times. This may have influenced the region's love of a pudding: there are hundreds of Kentish desserts, many incorporating fruit or the locally grown hazelnuts, also known as Kentish cobnuts. One creamy favourite is Kentish pudding pie (page 160), which is similar to a baked cheesecake.

The neighbouring county of Sussex has a quintessentially English steamed pudding named after it. Sussex pond pudding (page 158) is made with butter, brown sugar and lemon in a suet pastry case, the delicious dark oozy contents earning the dish its name. Substitute dried fruit for lemon, and the name changes to Kentish wells pudding. Other famous sweet fare from Sussex include lardy Johns and Sussex heavies. Across the border, Hampshire offers an equally intriguingly named dessert in the form of friar's

## Government, Greenwich and Gardens

London is, of course, the seat of Government in the UK, home to the Houses of Parliament and the major departments of state. Further East in London is the Royal Observatory, home of Greenwich Mean Time and the Prime Meridian line, one of the most important historic scientific sites in the world. It was founded by Charles II in 1675 and is the official starting point for each new day, year and millennium.

If you need a rest from all that politics and science, the region also boasts some of the most beautiful gardens in the country, from formal landscapes around stately homes to tiny cottage gardens. Examples include Sissinghurst Castle garden in Kent, created by Vita Sackville-West and her husband Sir Harold Nicolson,

both important figures in the world of garden design. The work of Gertrude Jekyll, another famous horticulturist, can be admired at Parham House in Sussex and Hatchlands Park in Surrey. One of the best-known figures in English gardening, 'Capability' Brown played a large part in the creation of the gardens of the magnificent Sussex stately homes Petworth House and Sheffield Park.

omelette, in which the soft flesh from baked apples is mixed with spices and egg yolk before being baked until set firm.

The coastline that surrounds the South East, together with the rivers that weave across it, provide an enormous amount of fish and shellfish. It is well known that oysters were once so ubiquitous that only the poor bothered to eat them, but other freshwater produce included eels and trout, while the sea offers shellfish, the delicate Dover sole and other flatfish.

What was once transported to be sold from London's fresh food markets now travels in to meet the capital's need for food. The abundant choice of the city's restaurants allows you to choose authentic fare from all around the globe. Whatever you are looking for, you are bound to find – and with a choice.

Finally, several dishes from this region rejoice in famous names. The strawberry, meringue and cream of Eton mess (page 148) was created for visiting parents to picnic on, while

**Above: Maids of honour (page 66) and, right, sumptuous sandwiches (page 54)**

Boodles orange fool (page 146) gets its name from the St James's club where it originated. London particular (page 30) is a pea and ham soup created by chefs at Simpson's in the Strand and named using the term for London's smog coined by Charles Dickens in his novel *Bleak House*. Brown Windsor soup bears the name of the royal castle in Berkshire.

# South West

INTRODUCTION

Think of the West Country and, for most of us, the mind turns to cream teas, seaside meals and cider. This tapering peninsula is warmed by the Gulf Stream, which makes the sea more welcoming and the climate so temperate that even tropical plants survive here.

Seafood is big business in Cornwall. Fishing boats set out for two seas from the long coastline and return with sardines, mackerel, monkfish, grey mullet and hake, as well as shellfish, crabs, crayfish and lobsters. The stargazy pie immortalised in children's books had pilchards' heads peeping out through the crust of the topping. Sadly, this evocative dish is rarely cooked today as the supply of these fish has become very erratic in the region.

The moors inland also host a variety of wild game such as rabbit and duck. The idea behind the ubiquitous Cornish pasty (page 50) was that the tin miners could hold it by the outer crust as they carried it to work, making it one of the earliest known fast (but certainly not junk) foods. What makes the Cornish pasty different from other pasties is that the ingredients were wrapped raw and then were subsequently cooked inside while the pastry was baked.

Moving northeast we arrive in cream tea heaven: Devon, where clotted cream is served with scones and a pot of tea. The county is also known for light yet rich little buns called Devonshire splits (there is a Cornish variety too), made using cream instead of milk.

The next county, Somerset, is the birthplace of the most famous cheese in Britain, the Cheddar, where it was matured in the caves of Cheddar Gorge from the fifteenth century. This creamy cheese can be flavoured from mild to strong and most of us reach for this variety when we need cheese for cooking purposes. It is also the basis for the ploughman's lunch (which was never actually eaten by ploughmen, but was a clever marketing device dating from the 1960s).

Cheddar's traditional companion, an apple, is also widely used in Somerset cooking (especially with pork) and, of course, can also be allowed to ferment into cider, another excellent cooking ingredient with pork and turkey. Somerset dairies also now produce the 'Queen of Cheeses', Brie, known for its smooth yet tangy taste and its lovely aroma.

If you are looking for an unusual recipe to drop into the conversation, try something from the next county to the east: Dorset. Choose between rook pie, a cheap dish for labourers, or the

## Seaside, Sir Francis Drake and cider

The coastline of the South West has many beaches, which attract holidaymakers in their thousands every summer. Families find that a trip with bucket and spade to the seaside keeps children of all ages happily occupied for many hours as they swim, sunbathe, dig and explore rock pools to find the secrets left at low tide.

This same coastline was the launching point for the first English circumnavigator of the globe, Sir Francis Drake. Born in 1545 in Tavistock, Devon, Drake is the most famous British naval adventurer of all time. It was from Plymouth that he set sail around the world in a journey eventually lasting three years from 1577, and to aid the defeat of the Spanish Armada in 1588.

Drake was a highly successful privateer (a sort of government-

sponsored pirate) and it is tempting to imagine that he began this practice of taking other people's property for his own in the many apple orchards of his native Devon. The windfalls from these orchards were traditionally made into scrumpy, or cider. Bruised and unsuitable for eating or cooking, the unripe fruits would be fermented into an alcoholic drink that is still an important West Country product.

Left: Cornish pasties (page 50) and, above, Cornish splits (page 64).

cabbages. Another old recipe (apparently dating from Victorian times at least) is for beef olives, which consist of thin sliced steak wrapped around a stuffing.

Finally, in our journey through the West Country, we reach Wiltshire, home of the lardy cake, named after the refined pig fat that gives delicious flavour to the white bread dough, sugar and dried fruit with which it is baked.

definitely more upmarket cygnets stuffed with beef, roasted in a flour and water paste. Dorset also has an interesting line in soups, including some made from lettuce, green peas or

# Wales

Wales is proudly different from neighbouring England, preserving its own language and culture. From harps, choirs and daffodils to the particular charms of the rugby pitch, Wales has many an icon to savour.

Over the centuries Wales has developed a simple and wholesome cuisine that reflects its sometimes challenging terrain and the tough demands of historic industries such as coal mining and steel making.

Much of the mountainous northern landscape can only sustain hardy oats and sheep, and these two ingredients appear in many guises in Welsh cooking. The southern terrain of valleys and rolling hills supports beef and dairy cattle and a wide variety of fruit, vegetables and cereal crops.

The meat most identified with Wales is lamb, its sweet flavour enhanced by mint, honey or lemon. However, beef cattle are also widely raised, and the traditional meat mainstay of the Welsh diet is the pig. Bacon appears in many Welsh recipes and indeed combines with lamb and sometimes beef as well in the famous dish called cawl. This is a classic one-pot meal (the word means 'broth' or 'soup') in which bacon is added to lamb scraps in a stock made from vegetables such as cabbage, swedes and potatoes. The national symbol of Wales, the leek – which, ironically, is not widely grown in the Principality – is sometimes added in small slices just before serving in one of the many variations on this hearty stew. Some families eat the soup with just vegetables in as an appetite-reducing first course before serving the meat element of the meal, and it is traditionally eaten with a wooden spoon.

Vegetables also feature heavily in the curiously named Glamorgan sausages (page 37), which are actually meat free, being a mixture of grated cheese, breadcrumbs with herbs and chopped leeks or onions. This thick paste is bound with egg and then rolled in flour to make sausage shapes, which are then fried and served with potatoes.

Cheese is the basis of another Welsh mainstay, Welsh rarebit, which has been adopted nationwide as a quick and easy snack. The simplest version is slices of cheese melted onto toast, but there are countless variations using a creamy blend of cheese with milk or cream plus butter or ale.

Just as leeks are more commonly grown outside Wales, so its most famous cheese, the crumbly and salty Caerphilly is

## Mountains, mines and music

Wales has a rich cultural and industrial history, and countless visitors go to this proud country to enjoy its spectacular scenery. Many head to Snowdonia in North Wales, known in Welsh as Eryri ('land of the eagles'), a region of plunging valleys and high peaks, tallest of which is the 3560ft (1085m) Snowdon itself. This, the highest peak south of the Scottish border, is particularly popular with walkers, climbers and mountain bikers.

Snowdonia is a landscape of wild moors, glacial lakes and dramatic waterfalls that has inspired visitors with its unchanging rocky beauty for centuries. The landscape of the south, in contrast, has altered dramatically in the last few decades as the pit wheels that marked the sites of collieries have been taken down and the vast coal pits filled in. Coal mining was once a major employer in South Wales, but the industry has now all but disappeared from the landscape.

Many miners used to meet after their shift to share their love of song and this tradition has thankfully survived. Many communities still boast a male voice choir and some tour to international acclaim with a repertoire of old traditional Welsh songs such as 'Men of Harlech' and 'Sospen fach'.

now mainly produced over the border in the West Country. However, Welsh dairies do produce a range of cheeses including goats' cheeses and some fine Cheddar.

The seas and rivers of Wales host a range of fish, including the sewin (Welsh for sea trout), traditionally baked wrapped in bacon (page 103). However, one of the most noteworthy products of the sea is the edible seaweed harvested and used to create an unusual breakfast dish. Laver is collected from the rocks, washed and boiled for hours to form a purée, which is mixed with fine oatmeal to form small cakes that are fried in bacon fat.

Finally, there is a wealth of tea-time treats in the list of Welsh fare, from oven-baked

**Above: Welsh leek soup (page 27); above right: Glamorgan sausages (page 37) and, right, Monmouth pudding (page 157)**

bara brith (page 76) to melt-in-the-mouth delicacies from the griddle such as Welsh cakes and crempog, which are very rich pancakes made with buttermilk.

# Lazy lunches

Enjoy a satisfying snack such as London particular or Gloucester cheese and ale. When time allows, linger over a sociable lunch or picnic, savouring the delights of ploughman's with chutney, Glamorgan sausages or Cornish pasties. You'll find a recipe for all lunchtime occasions.

# Parsnip and apple soup

This creamy soup originates from East Anglia, where root crops thrive in the fertile soil. The sweet and velvety texture of parsnip combines wonderfully with a hint of tart cooking apple. Blended with cream, this is a really smooth starter.

**Butter** 25g (1oz)

**Parsnips** 680g (1½lb), peeled and sliced

**Bramley cooking apple** 1, cored, peeled and sliced

**Vegetable stock** 1.25 litres (2 pints)

**Sage leaves** 4, plus extra to garnish

**Cloves** 2

**Single cream** 150ml (5fl oz)

**Salt and freshly ground black pepper**

**Dessert apple** 1, cored, peeled, sliced and fried in 25g (1oz) butter, to garnish

## Cook's tips

• If you prefer, use ½ tsp of dried sage when cooking the parsnips.

• For a lower fat version, simply omit the cream – the soup still tastes really good.

| | |
|---|---|
| Preparation time | 10 minutes |
| Cooking time | 40 minutes |
| Calories per portion | 172 Kcal |
| Fat per portion | 10g |
| of which saturated | 5.2g |
| Serves | 6 |
| Suitable for vegetarians | |
| Suitable for freezing | |

1 Melt the butter in a large saucepan and add the parsnips and apple. Cover and cook gently for 10 minutes, stirring occasionally.

2 Pour the stock into the saucepan and add the sage and cloves. Bring to the boil, cover and then simmer for 30 minutes, until the parsnip is softened.

3 Remove the sage leaves and cloves, then purée the parsnips in a blender or food processor.

4 Return to the saucepan and reheat gently with the cream. Season to taste. Serve hot, garnished with the sage leaves and apple slices and with granary bread.

# Welsh leek soup

As the national emblem of Wales, leeks are used in many of the region's recipes. This soup is also known as *cawl cennin*, the word 'cawl' meaning broth. Leeks are available virtually all year round and as this soup is quick to make, enjoy it as often as you like!

**Butter** 25g (1oz)

**Onion** 1, peeled and chopped

**Potato** 1, peeled and diced

**Celery** 2 sticks, chopped

**Leeks** 3, trimmed, sliced and washed

**Stock, chicken or vegetable** 900ml (1½ pints)

**Salt and freshly ground black pepper**

**Crème fraîche** 6 tbsp (about half a tub) plus extra for serving

**Chives** to garnish

1 Heat the butter in a large saucepan and add the onion, potato and celery. Cook over a medium heat for 5 minutes, stirring a couple of times.

2 Add the leeks to the pan, cover and cook for 10 minutes, stirring occasionally.

3 Add the stock and some seasoning and simmer, half-covered with the lid, for 20 minutes or until the potato is softened.

4 Ladle out about half the soup into a food processor and purée until fairly smooth. Pour the purée back into the pan with the rest of the soup and reheat with the crème fraîche. Add hot water to thin the soup a little more if you like.

5 Serve hot in warmed bowls, each garnished with a spoonful of crème fraîche and some snipped chives.

## Cook's tips

• Purée the whole batch of soup if you prefer it all smooth.

• Freeze the soup in manageable portions – don't forget to leave space in the container for expansion.

• If you haven't got crème fraîche, use double or single cream instead.

| | |
|---|---|
| Preparation time | 10 minutes |
| Cooking time | 40 minutes |
| Calories per portion | 140 Kcal |
| Fat per portion | 11g |
| of which saturated | 6.5g |
| Serves | 6 |
| Suitable for vegetarians (with vegetable stock) | |
| Suitable for freezing | |

# Cullen skink

The name of this rich, tasty soup comes from the fishing village of Cullen, in Morayshire. 'Skink' is a soup made originally from a shin of beef. In this case, the main ingredient is smoked haddock.

**Finnan haddock** 1 (about 900g/2lb) or 500g (1lb 2oz) un-dyed smoked haddock fillet

**Onion** 1 large, skinned and thinly sliced

**Milk** 600ml (1 pint)

**Potatoes suitable for mashing (such as King Edwards)** 680g (1½lb), peeled and thickly sliced

**Leeks** 2, trimmed, thinly sliced and washed

**Butter** 40g (1½oz), cut into small pieces

**Salt and freshly ground black pepper**

**Mace** to garnish

**Parsley** sprigs, to garnish

1 Place the haddock in a large saucepan, add the onion, milk and 600ml (1 pint) of water. Bring to the boil, then reduce the heat, cover and cook gently for 10 minutes, or until the flesh flakes easily.

2 While the fish is cooking, place the potatoes in another large saucepan, cover with water, add ½ tsp of salt and bring to the boil. Then reduce the heat, partially cover the pan and cook until tender. Drain the cooked potatoes, and then mash them well with a potato masher.

3 Place a large colander over a bowl. Pour the haddock into the colander and leave it to drain well, and until cool enough to handle. Reserve the cooking liquid.

4 Remove and discard skin and bones from the fish, then flake the flesh. Reserve the onion.

5 Pour the fish liquid back into a clean pan, then using a balloon or hand whisk, gradually whisk in the mashed potatoes. Add the leeks and bring back to the boil, then reduce the heat, cover and cook gently for 10–15 minutes until the leeks are tender.

6 Gradually stir the butter into the soup, season to taste with salt and pepper, and then add the flaked fish and reserved onion. Cook gently for 5 minutes, or until the haddock is thoroughly reheated, taking care not to overheat as the fish will become tough.

7 Serve the soup in warm bowls, sprinkled with mace, black pepper and parsley leaves, and accompanied with warm crusty bread.

## Cook's tip

• For a richer flavoured soup, use fresh fish stock instead of water.

| | |
|---|---|
| Preparation time | 30 minutes |
| Cooking time | 40 minutes |
| Calories per portion | 411 Kcal |
| Fat per portion | 12g |
| of which saturated | 6.9g |
| Serves | 4 |

LAZY LUNCHES

# London particular

This gloriously green soup got its name from the thick fogs known as 'pea-soupers' that used to blanket London in centuries gone by. It is still the perfect comfort food to warm you up on a gloomy day.

**Split dried peas** 450g (1lb)
**Rindless streaky bacon** 3 rashers, chopped
**Onion** 1, peeled and roughly chopped
**Carrot** 1, peeled and diced
**Celery** 1 stick, chopped
**Chicken or ham stock** 2.5 litres (4 pints)
**Salt and freshly ground black pepper**
**Double cream** 6 tbsp, optional
**Grilled bacon** chopped, to garnish

1 If the dried peas need soaking, do this first, following the manufacturer's instructions. Put the bacon, onion, carrot and celery in a large saucepan and cook for 5–10 minutes, until beginning to soften.

2 Add the peas and stock and bring to the boil. Boil rapidly, uncovered for 10 minutes, then cover and simmer for around an hour, until the peas are tender.

3 Allow to cool slightly, then purée in a blender or food processor, until smooth.

4 Return the soup to the pan. Season to taste, and reheat gently. Serve hot, with a swirl of cream, if using, and garnished with the chopped bacon.

## Cook's tip

• For a vegetarian version, omit the bacon and replace the meat stock with vegetable stock.

| | |
|---|---|
| Preparation time | 10 minutes plus possible soaking time |
| Cooking time | 20 minutes |
| Calories per portion | 308 Kcal |
| Fat per portion | 5g |
| of which saturated | 1.8g |
| Serves | 6 |
| Suitable for freezing | |

# Cock-a-leekie soup

This famous Scottish soup – 'a pullet with some prunes in the broth' – is the traditional starter for a Burns Supper (see page 174 for main course). The original recipe included leftover beef, so feel free to add some. But do it towards the end so it doesn't toughen.

**Chicken breasts** 350g (12oz)
**Unsalted butter** 15g (½oz)
**Leeks** 350g (12oz), trimmed
**Chicken stock** 1.25 litres (2 pints)
**Bouquet garni** 1
**Salt and freshly ground black pepper**
**Ready to eat prunes** 8, stoned and halved

1 Wash the chicken and pat dry. Melt the butter in a large saucepan and fry the chicken for 4–5 minutes until golden on all sides.

2 Cut the white part of the leeks into four lengthways and chop into 2.5cm (1in) pieces, reserving the green parts. Wash well. Add the white parts to the pan and fry for 2–3 minutes until soft.

3 Add the stock and bouquet garni and season to taste. Bring to the boil and simmer for 30 minutes or until the chicken is tender.

4 Shred the reserved green parts of the leeks, reserve a few for garnish, then add to the pan with the prunes. Simmer for a further 35 minutes.

5 To serve, remove the chicken and cut the meat into large pieces. Put the meat in a warmed soup tureen and pour in the soup. Serve hot, garnished with the reserved leek.

## Cook's tip

• If you want to serve the soup as a main meal, add 225g (8oz) cooked pearl barley or rice when you add the prunes.

| | |
|---|---|
| Preparation time | 10 minutes |
| Cooking time | 45 minutes |
| Calories per portion | 176 Kcal |
| Fat per portion | 5g |
| of which saturated | 2.3g |
| Serves | 4 |

# Ploughmans with chutney

We are all familiar with the 'Ploughman's lunch', which would suggest that it is an ancient term. However, it would seem that the term did not appear until the 1960s, dreamt up by some clever advertising executive to promote the traditional pub lunch.

**Cooking apples** 1.8kg (4lb), peeled, cored and roughly chopped

**Onions** 900g (2lb), peeled, halved and thickly sliced lengthways

**Dry cider** 500ml (18fl oz)

**Sultanas** 175g (6oz)

**Seedless raisins** 175g (6oz)

**Salt** 25g (1oz)

**Ground ginger** 15g (½oz)

**Sweet paprika** 1 tbsp

**Clear honey** 225g (8oz)

**Soft dark brown sugar** 110g (4oz)

**Distilled malt vinegar** 900ml (1½ pints)

**Wholemeal bread, Cheddar cheese, salad** to accompany the chutney

1 Place the apples and onions in a large, heavy-based preserving pan. Add the cider and cook over a moderate heat for 20 minutes, until the apples and onions start to soften.

2 Add the sultanas, raisins, salt, ginger, paprika, honey and sugar to the pan. Pour in half of the vinegar, stir well and cook for 20 minutes.

3 Stir in the remaining vinegar and bring to the boil, stirring occasionally. Then reduce the heat and allow the chutney to cook at a gentle bubble until reduced by approximately two-thirds, or until when a spoon drawn through the centre leaves a gap that is slow to close up. Stir the chutney frequently to prevent it burning.

4 Remove the pan from the heat and allow the chutney to cool until cold, then spoon into clean jars. Using a clean skewer, work the skewer backwards and forwards through the chutney to remove any air bubbles.

5 Wipe the tops of the jars clean, and then cover with acid-proof lids. Store in a cool, dark, dry and airy cupboard. Preferably, allow the chutney to mature for two to three months before using.

## Cook's tip

• Cheddar cheese is the traditional accompaniment for a ploughmans lunch; but don't feel that you should limit yourself to Cheddar alone. There are a great many delicious British cheeses out there – see pages 168-171.

Preparation time – 1 hour
Cooking time – 3–3½ hours
Calories per tablespoon – 36 Kcal
Fat per tablespoon – 0g
Makes – 2.3kg (5lb)
Suitable for vegetarians

# Cheese and apple parcels

Sweet juicy apple goes well with this tangy regional cheese in a puff pastry case. Quick to make using ready-made puff pastry, these parcels make great picnic food. Serve with a herb and leaf salad.

**Ready-made puff pastry** 500g pack
**Egg** 1, beaten to glaze
**Cheshire cheese** 175g (6oz)
**Dessert apples** 1 large, peeled, quartered, cored and cut into small dice
**Chopped parsley** 4 tbsp
**Salt and freshly ground black pepper**

1 Preheat the oven to 220°C/425°F/Gas 7. Make the filling. Crumble the cheese into a bowl and mix the apple into the cheese with the parsley and seasoning.

2 Roll out half the pack of pastry thinly on a lightly floured surface and, using a saucer or bowl as a guide, cut out four, 12cm (5in) rounds. Stack the trimmings on top of each other then roll them out and cut out another two rounds.

3 Brush the edges of the circles with a little beaten egg then spoon some filling onto one side of each of the rounds. Fold the other side over the filling and press the edges together well to seal. Knock up the edges with a knife blade then flute them.

4 Place the pastries on a baking sheet and brush with beaten egg. Score each pastry three to four times across the top. Bake for 15–20 minutes until risen and golden.

5 While the first batch of pastries is cooking, roll out the rest of the pastry and make the second batch, as above. Serve warm with salad.

## Cook's tips

• Use a 600ml (1 pint) pudding basin as a size guide for cutting the pastry.
• Cooking one batch at a time ensures a better rise for all the pastries rather than switching trays over halfway through cooking.

| | |
|---|---|
| Preparation time | 20 minutes |
| Cooking time | 40 minutes |
| Calories per parcel | 226 Kcal |
| Fat per parcel | 15g |
| of which saturated | 6.9g |
| Makes | 12 parcels |
| Suitable for vegetarians | |

# Gloucester cheese and ale

An English variation of Welsh rarebit, this filling snack was originally served after the meat course of the evening meal at inns or posting houses. These days, it is perfect for a light lunch, served with a tomato salad and a glass of real ale.

**Brown ale** 150ml (¼ pint)
**Double Gloucester cheese** 175g (6oz), grated
**English mustard** 1 tsp
**Cornflour** 2 tsp, blended in 1 tsp of water
**Wholemeal bread** 4 thick slices

1 Pour the brown ale into a saucepan and add the cheese, mustard and cornflour. Heat gently until the cheese has melted and the sauce thickens.

2 Meanwhile, toast the bread. Pour the warm ale and cheese over the toast (you might like to grill for a little extra colour at this stage), season to taste, and serve immediately.

## Cook's tip

• Take care not to overheat, or the cheese and ale mixture may separate.

Preparation time – 5 minutes
Cooking time – 10 minutes
Calories per portion – 290 Kcal
Fat per portion – 16g
of which saturated – 9.6g
Serves – 4
Suitable for vegetarians

# Brie with redcurrant jelly

Made in Somerset, according to traditional French methods, Somerset brie is considered by many to be as fine as French brie, with its straw colour and creamy tangy flavour. Serve it coated in breadcrumbs, as a really simple, light lunch – delicious!

**Somerset brie** 150g (5oz)
**Egg** 1, beaten
**Fresh wholemeal breadcrumbs** 50g (2oz)
**Butter** 25g (1oz)
**Vegetable oil** 1 tbsp
**Redcurrant jelly** 2 tbsp
**Water** 1 tbsp
**Curly endive lettuce** to serve
**Redcurrants** to garnish

## Cook's tip

• Ensure the cheese is well chilled, otherwise it may melt before the breadcrumbs are crispy.

| | |
|---|---|
| Preparation time | 5 minutes |
| Cooking time | 5 minutes |
| Calories per portion | 271 Kcal |
| Fat per portion | 21g |
| of which saturated | 10.5g |
| Serves | 4 |
| Suitable for vegetarians | |

1 Cut the cheese into four equal-sized slices. Dip in the beaten egg and coat in the breadcrumbs.

2 Heat the butter and oil in a large frying pan and fry the cheese slices for about 10 seconds on each side, until the breadcrumbs are crispy and golden. Drain on kitchen paper.

3 Meanwhile, put the redcurrant jelly and 1 tbsp of water in a saucepan and heat gently until the jelly melts.

4 Place each cheese slice on a bed of lettuce and drizzle with redcurrant sauce. Garnish with the redcurrants and serve immediately.

# Pan haggerty

The name of this favourite Geordie supper dish was originally one word, Panhaggerty, meaning onions and potatoes. It is a one-pan dish, which may be served on its own with salad or as an accompaniment to a main meal, such as sausages or grilled chops.

**Butter** 25g (1oz)
**Sunflower oil** 1 tbsp
**Potatoes** 500g (1lb 2oz), peeled and thinly sliced
**Onion** 1, peeled and sliced
**Lancashire cheese** 110g (4oz), grated
**Salt and freshly ground black pepper**

## Cook's tip

• If your Pan haggerty is not to be a vegetarian dish, try adding some chopped ham or bacon to the layers to make more of a main meal dish.

| | |
|---|---|
| Preparation time | 10 minutes |
| Cooking time | 35 minutes |
| Calories per portion (2 servings) | 558 Kcal |
| Fat per portion (2 servings) | 33g |
| of which saturated | 18.1g |
| Serves | 2 as main meal |
| | 4 as accompaniment |
| Suitable for vegetarians | |

1 Heat the butter and oil in a solid-based frying pan until the butter has melted.

2 Starting with a layer of potatoes and finishing with a layer of cheese, layer up the potatoes, onion and cheese, seasoning each layer well.

3 Cover the pan either with a lid or foil, and cook over a gentle heat for 20–30 minutes, or until the potato and onion are tender when pierced with the point of a fine knife.

4 Remove the cover and cook under a hot grill to brown the top. Serve the dish straight from the pan.

# Glamorgan sausages

Originally a poor man's meat substitute for the real thing, nowadays these cheesy delicacies are perfect for a vegetarian lunch. Serve the sausages with lots of salad for a hearty and satisfying snack.

**Breadcrumbs** 175g (6oz)
**Caerphilly cheese** 110g (4oz), grated
**Leek** 1 small, trimmed, washed and very finely chopped
**Chopped parsley** 1 tbsp
**Mustard powder** ½ tsp
**Salt and freshly ground black pepper**
**Eggs** 2, 1 separated
**Milk** 4 tbsp
**Plain flour** 2 tbsp
**Vegetable oil** 1 tbsp
**Butter** 15g (½oz)
**Tomatoes** sliced, to serve
**Parsley** to garnish

1 In a large bowl combine the breadcrumbs, cheese, leek, parsley and mustard. Season to taste. Add 1 whole egg and 1 egg yolk and mix thoroughly. If necessary, add enough milk to bind the mixture together.

2 Divide the mixture into eight and shape into sausages about 10cm (4in) long.

3 On a large plate, beat the remaining egg white with a fork until frothy. Place the sausages on the plate and brush the egg white all over them, until evenly coated. Roll the sausages in the flour.

4 Heat the oil and butter in a frying pan and fry the sausages for 5–10 minutes, turning occasionally, until golden brown. Serve hot or cold on a bed of sliced tomato and with a sprig of parsley.

## Cook's tip

• For a vegetarian main meal, serve with potato wedges and a large salad.

| | |
|---|---|
| Preparation time | 10 minutes |
| Cooking time | 10 minutes |
| Calories per portion | 397 Kcal |
| Fat per portion | 19g |
| of which saturated | 8.8g |
| Serves | 4 |
| Suitable for vegetarians | |
| Suitable for freezing | |

37

# Smoked trout pâté

This wonderfully simple recipe originates from Great Yarmouth, home of the bloater. It is perfect for a light lunch or as a starter to a main meal.

**Smoked trout fillet** 3 x 125g packets, flaked and bones removed

**Butter** 50g (2oz), softened

**Lemon juice** 3 tbsp

**Single cream** 6 tbsp

**Freshly ground black pepper**

**Ground mace** ½ tsp, plus extra to garnish

**Lemon slices** to garnish

**1** Put the trout flesh in a blender or food processor. Add the butter, lemon juice, cream, pepper and mace and blend until smooth.

**2** Divide the pâté between four or six ramekin dishes and chill for an hour. Garnish with mace, black pepper and slices of lemon and serve with fingers of wholemeal toast.

## Cook's tip

• If you do not have a food processor, mash together the ingredients with a fork.

| | |
|---|---|
| Preparation time | 30 minutes |
| Calories per portion | 251 Kcal |
| Fat per portion | 19g |
| of which saturated | 10.2g |
| Serves | 4 |

# Scotch woodcock

Scotch woodcock may refer to the class distinction between the 'have and have nots' – those who could afford to eat real woodcock and those who had to make do with eggs!

**Eggs** 4
**Egg yolks** 4
**Single cream** 300ml (½ pint)
**Salt and freshly ground black pepper**
**Unsalted butter** 50g (2oz), softened
**White bread** 4 slices
**Anchovy fillets in olive oil** 8 fillets, drained
**Capers in brine** 16, drained
**Chopped parsley** 2 tbsp

1 In a mixing bowl, beat together the eggs, egg yolks and cream and season lightly.

2 Melt half the butter in a saucepan until bubbling and pour in the egg mixture. Cook over a low heat, stirring, for about 4 minutes, until the mixture 'scrambles'.

3 Toast the bread on both sides, remove the crusts if preferred, and spread with the remaining butter.

4 To serve, pile the scrambled egg on top of each piece of toast and arrange anchovy fillets as a cross on each one, topped with four capers. Sprinkle with chopped parsley and serve with grilled tomatoes and gently fried mushrooms.

## Cook's tip

• You may prefer to mash the anchovies with the softened butter before spreading on the toast instead of using whole fillets on top of the egg – you will need an extra 25g (1oz) butter for this variation.

| | |
|---|---|
| Preparation time | 10 minutes |
| Cooking time | 7 minutes |
| Calories per portion | 487 Kcal |
| Fat per portion | 39g |
| of which saturated | 19.4g |
| Serves | 4 |

# Morecambe Bay potted shrimps

Morecambe Bay shrimps have been caught by local fishermen from Flookburgh, Ulverston, Bardsea and along the coast road to Rampside for hundreds of years. Traditionally, small brown shrimps are used in this recipe, but any peeled shrimps or prawns will work well.

**Butter** 110g (4oz)

**Shrimps** 250–300g (9–11oz), shelled weight

**Ground nutmeg** pinch

**Ground mace** pinch

**Salt and freshly ground black pepper**

## Cook's tips

• The ramekins look pretty garnished with sprigs of dill and, for special occasions, a little caviar.

• The shrimps are usually covered with a layer of butter to seal them in the ramekin dishes. To keep the fat content lower, this recipe uses slightly less butter than usual and the prawns may show through the top. Extra clarified butter may be used if you want the shrimps to be completely covered.

| | |
|---|---|
| Preparation time | 10 minutes |
| Cooking time | 5 minutes |
| Calories per portion | 281 Kcal |
| Fat per portion | 21g |
| of which saturated | 14.5g |
| Serves | 4 |

1 Melt the butter gently in a saucepan and then leave it to set for 10–15 minutes in the fridge. Remove the clarified butter layer from the top and discard the runny liquid underneath.

2 Melt half of the clarified butter and stir in the shrimps, nutmeg, mace and seasoning to taste. Divide the mixture between four small ramekin dishes. Chill the dishes until the mixture has set.

3 Melt the remaining clarified butter and spoon over the top of the dishes. Chill the ramekins until the mixture has set.

4 Serve with toast or crusty brown bread, using the butter layer on top of the ramekins to spread on the toast first.

# Herrings in oatmeal

Here is a very healthy dish, rich in omega-3 fatty acids and fibre. Herrings or mackerel are simple to prepare, nutritious and delicious. If you can't get hold of herrings, use mackerel instead. Oatmeal is available from any health food shop.

**Herrings** 2, cleaned, heads and tails removed
**Salt and freshly ground black pepper**
**Medium oatmeal** 50g (2oz)
**Vegetable oil** 1 tbsp
**Lemon wedges** to serve

1 To remove the backbone of the fish, put on a board cut side down. Press lightly with your fingers down the middle of the back. Turn the fish over and ease up the backbone. Fold the fish in half. Season well and coat with the oatmeal.

2 Heat the oil in a large frying pan and fry the herrings for 4–5 minutes on each side. Drain well, cut in half and serve hot with the lemon wedges and a crispy salad.

## Cook's tip

• Ask your fishmonger to prepare the herrings for you but you still may need to check for bones.

| | |
|---|---|
| Preparation time | 10 minutes |
| Cooking time | 10 minutes |
| Calories per portion | 378 Kcal |
| Fat per portion | 24g |
| of which saturated | 3.7g |
| Serves | 2 |
| Suitable for freezing | |

# Mackerel salad with gooseberries

This salad is based on a classic combination of freshly caught grilled mackerel and locally grown juicy gooseberries, popular in the West Country. It makes a great alternative to prawn cocktail as a starter for six to eight people or a satisfying lunch for four.

**Baby new potatoes** 680g (1½lb), scrubbed
**Salt**
**Gooseberries** 225g (8oz)
**Caster sugar** 25g (1oz)
**Apple juice** 3 tbsp
**Raspberry vinegar** 3 tbsp
**Mini cucumber** 1
**Radishes** 110g (4oz)
**Mackerel fillets** 8 x 110g (4oz)
**Wholegrain mustard** 1 tbsp
**Clear honey** 1 tbsp
**Mixed baby salad leaves** 50g (2oz)

1 Halve the potatoes and place in a large saucepan with a pinch of salt. Cover with water, bring to the boil and cook for 10–12 minutes until tender. Drain well and allow to cool.

2 Meanwhile, top and tail the gooseberries, and place in a small saucepan with the sugar, apple juice and raspberry vinegar. Heat gently until the sugar dissolves, then bring to the boil, cover and simmer gently for 3–4 minutes until soft. Set aside to cool.

3 Trim and thinly slice the cucumber and radishes. Place in a bowl, cover and chill until required.

4 Wash and pat dry the mackerel fillets. Mix together the mustard and honey. Preheat a grill to a medium/hot setting. Arrange the mackerel fillets, flesh side up, on the grill rack and brush with mustard and honey. Cook, without turning, for 5–6 minutes until tender and cooked through. Drain and keep warm.

5 To serve, either mash the gooseberry mixture with a fork or place in a blender or food processor and blend until smooth. Pile salad leaves on four serving plates. Mix the potatoes with the cucumber and radishes and pile on top. Arrange two fillets per salad and serve with the gooseberry dressing spooned over.

## Cook's tip

• Raspberry vinegar gives an extra fruity note to this sweet and sour dressing, but red wine vinegar would work just as well, although you may want to add a little more sugar. Replace gooseberries with raspberries if preferred.

| | |
|---|---|
| Preparation time | 20 minutes |
| Cooking time | 20 minutes |
| Calories per portion | 668 Kcal |
| Fat per portion | 37g |
| of which saturated | 7.2g |
| Serves | 4 |

# 'Twice laid'

The delightful title of this Kentish recipe for using up leftover fish and potatoes is far more enticing than today's terminology – 'using up leftovers'! 'Twice laid' is so-called because the fish and potatoes are being placed on the table for a second time.

**Haddock or cod** 680g (1½lb) fresh or smoked (un-dyed) (cooked weight if using leftover fish 350g/12oz)

**Bay leaves** 3

**Black peppercorns** 1 tsp

**Salt** ½ tsp

**Lemon** ½, thinly sliced, plus wedges for serving

**Potatoes** 680g (1½lb), peeled and diced (if using leftover cooked potatoes 500g/1lb 2oz)

**Butter** 25g (1oz), melted

**Chopped parsley** 3 tbsp

**Finely snipped chives** 2 tbsp

**Salt and freshly ground black pepper**

**Egg** 1 large, beaten

**White breadcrumbs**

**Corn oil** 1 litre bottle, for deep-frying

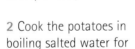

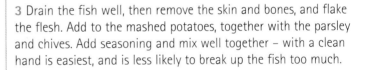

## Safety tips

• Only fill the pan a third full with oil. Never add too much food to the hot oil, as it can cause the oil to rise and overflow. Preferably, place the pan on a gas or electric ring or solid hot plate at the back of the hob.

• Keep the kitchen paper for draining well away from the hob.

• When deep fat frying, have a large wet tea towel within reach in case the oil catches fire. Should this happen, turn off the heat immediately and cover the pan with the tea towel. NEVER attempt to move the pan.

| Preparation time | 1½ hours |
|---|---|
| Cooking time | 20 minutes |
| Calories per portion | 672 Kcal |
| Fat per portion | 31g |
| of which saturated | 6.9g |
| Serves | 4 |

1 Rinse the fish under cold water and then place it in a large shallow saucepan. Add the bay leaves, peppercorns, salt and lemon slices. Cover with water and bring to the boil, then remove from the heat and leave to cool while the potatoes are cooking – during which time the fish will cook perfectly.

2 Cook the potatoes in boiling salted water for 20–25 minutes, until cooked. Drain well, transfer to a large bowl, add the butter and mash well. Set aside to cool.

3 Drain the fish well, then remove the skin and bones, and flake the flesh. Add to the mashed potatoes, together with the parsley and chives. Add seasoning and mix well together – with a clean hand is easiest, and is less likely to break up the fish too much.

4 Pour the beaten egg onto a plate and spread out the breadcrumbs on a baking tray or large plate.

5 Divide the fish and potato mixture into 12 equal pieces and shape each one into a ball. Then, one at a time, brush the balls with beaten egg and carefully roll in the breadcrumbs until evenly coated.

6 Deep-fry the fish cakes in hot oil, in batches of four, for 4–5 minutes until golden brown. Remove from the pan with a slotted spoon, drain on kitchen paper and keep hot until all the fish cakes are cooked. Serve immediately, accompanied with a fresh, crisp green salad.

# Mock game

When game is unavailable, this Warwickshire method of braising meat with spices, stock and wine is a good alternative, as it very closely resembles the flavour of pheasant. It can be made with beaten slices of steak rolled up with bacon or, as here, with chicken breasts.

**Skinless chicken breasts** 8, approximately 150g (5oz) each

**Dry-cured smoked bacon** 8 rashers, rinds removed

**Salt and freshly ground black pepper**

**Butter** 50g (2oz)

**Olive oil** 1 tbsp

**Red wine** 225ml (8fl oz)

**Chicken stock** 300ml (10fl oz)

**Lemon** 1, thinly pared rind only

**Redcurrant jelly** 6 tbsp

**Allspice berries** ½ tsp

**Black peppercorns** ½ tsp

**Cloves** 2–3

**Bay leaves** 2–3

**Plain flour** 25g (1oz)

**Chopped parsley** 3 tbsp

**Brown or white bread** 8 thin slices

1 Using a meat mallet or rolling pin, beat each chicken breast thinly between two sheets of cling film. With the back of a knife, gently stretch out each rasher of bacon to the same length as each chicken breast.

2 Place the chicken breasts skinned side down on a board and season well. Place a bacon rasher on each one and roll up neatly – starting at the wider end. Tie each 'parcel' with clean string.

3 Heat half of the butter with the olive oil in a large flameproof casserole or a lidded frying pan. Add the parcels and cook gently until lightly browned all over. Remove from pan and set aside.

4 Pour the wine into the casserole and bring to the boil, stirring and scraping the browned residue from the bottom, then boil gently until the wine is reduced by a third.

5 Add the chicken stock, lemon rind, half the redcurrant jelly, allspice berries, peppercorns, cloves and bay leaves. Return the chicken to the pan and bring back to the boil. Reduce the heat and cover the surface closely with greaseproof paper. Cover with its lid and cook gently for 25–30 minutes until the chicken is cooked.

6 Meanwhile, blend the remaining butter with the flour to make a soft paste.

7 When cooked, use a slotted spoon to transfer the paupiettes from the casserole onto a plate. Then remove the string from each one and arrange in a warmed serving dish. Cover and keep warm while finishing the sauce.

8 A little at a time, gradually whisk the butter and flour mixture into the sauce remaining in the casserole, and bring back to the boil – stirring with the whisk. Reduce the heat and simmer gently while preparing the toasts.

9 Mix together the chopped parsley and the remaining redcurrant jelly. Toast the bread on both sides and spread each slice with the redcurrant and parsley jelly. Cut off and discard the crusts, then cut each slice into quarters and keep warm. Through a fine sieve, carefully strain the sauce over the parcels. Serve accompanied with the prepared toasts.

## Cook's tip

• For a more substantial meal, serve with sautéed potatoes and cooked red cabbage.

| | |
|---|---|
| Preparation time | 45 minutes |
| Cooking time | 30 minutes |
| Calories per portion | 752 Kcal |
| Fat per portion | 27g |
| of which saturated | 12g |
| Serves | 4 |

45

# All-day breakfast salad

There's nothing like Scottish black pudding, and many butchers have their own 'secret' recipes for it, but it's not just for breakfast. Combined with other traditional breakfast ingredients, this salad is suitable for a light lunch or supper, too.

**Olive oil** 6 tbsp
**Streaky bacon** 6 rashers
**Black pudding** 170g packet, sliced
**Quail eggs** 12
**Mixed salad leaves** 175-200g (6-7oz)
**Cider vinegar** 1 tbsp
**Caster sugar** 1 tsp
**Mustard powder** ½ tsp
**Salt and freshly ground black pepper**

1 Heat 1 tbsp of the olive oil in a frying pan, add the bacon and cook for 3-4 minutes until it starts to crisp. Remove from the pan and cut into strips. Then add the black pudding and fry for 1-2 minutes on each side until cooked through.

2 Cook the quail eggs in boiling water for 3 minutes. Meanwhile, divide the salad leaves between four plates and scatter the black pudding and bacon over the top.

3 Drain and peel the quail eggs (although you could leave on the shell for colour interest), cut them in half and arrange them on the salad leaves.

4 To make the dressing, whisk the remaining olive oil with the cider vinegar, sugar and mustard powder, season to taste. Drizzle the dressing over the salads and serve immediately while the topping ingredients are still warm. Serve with crusty bread.

## Cook's tip

• Instead of using quail eggs, use four hard-boiled ordinary eggs, quarter them lengthways and arrange on the salad.

| | |
|---|---|
| Preparation time | 15 minutes |
| Cooking time | 10 minutes |
| Calories per portion | 442 Kcal |
| Fat per portion | 37g |
| of which saturated | 5.2g |
| Serves | 4 |

# Watercress and bacon salad

Peppery watercress from Hampshire beds contrasts beautifully with tender new potatoes. The crispy bacon adds a crunchy texture and salty flavour. This salad is perfect eaten outdoors while enjoying the first rays of summer sunshine and crops of new potatoes.

LAZY LUNCHES

**Small new potatoes** 450g (1lb), scrubbed

**Olive oil** 3 tbsp

**White wine vinegar** 1 tbsp

**Wholegrain mustard** 1 tbsp

**Clear honey** 2 tsp

**Salt and freshly ground black pepper**

**Unsmoked lean back bacon** 8 rashers, chopped

**Watercress** 1 bunch, trimmed and roughly chopped

## Cook's tip

• If you cannot obtain watercress, try mixed green salad or rocket.

| | |
|---|---|
| Preparation time | 10 minutes |
| Cooking time | 20 minutes |
| Calories per portion | 239 Kcal |
| Fat per portion | 13g |
| of which saturated | 2.4g |
| Serves | 4 |

1 Cook the potatoes in salted boiling water for 10–15 minutes, until tender.

2 Meanwhile, mix together the oil, vinegar, mustard and honey, season and set aside. Fry the bacon in its own fat for 5 minutes, until cooked and drain on kitchen paper.

3 Drain the cooked potatoes and mix with the bacon. Serve warm on a bed of watercress with the dressing.

47

# Scotch eggs

These eggs used to be served as part of a Scottish breakfast after the porridge with whisky. More familiar today as part of a picnic lunch, this version is for those who like homemade Scotch eggs but don't enjoy having to breadcrumb the eggs and then deep fry them.

**Eggs** 6
**White bread,** 2 slices, crusts removed
**Milk** 4 tbsp
**Cumberland sausages** 500g (1lb 2oz)
**Chopped parsley** 2 tbsp
**Grated nutmeg**
**Salt and freshly ground black pepper**
**Streaky bacon** 6 rashers, de-rinded and stretched

1 Add the eggs to a saucepan of boiling water. Bring back to the boil and simmer for 5 minutes from the moment the water starts to bubble. Drain, then cool under cold running water.

2 Preheat the oven to 190°C/375°F/Gas 5 and have a six-hole deep muffin tin ready. Shell the eggs, wash and set aside.

3 Put the bread in a large bowl, add the milk and leave for 2 minutes for it to soak in, then mash it down with your hand – this makes it easier to mix with the rest of the ingredients.

4 Split the skins on the sausages and put the meat into the bowl with the soaked bread and discard the skins. Add the parsley, a good grating of nutmeg and seasoning. Work everything together with your hand. Divide the mixture into six balls then flatten them to make rounds.

5 Stand a boiled egg in the middle of each round, pointed end up, and work the meat up around the egg to form a smooth, even layer, sealing the egg completely.

6 Put each egg in a hole in the muffin tin then criss-cross two pieces of bacon over the top, tucking in the loose ends.

7 Bake for 35 minutes. Leave for 5 minutes in the tin and then run a knife around to get them out. Drain on kitchen paper for a few minutes. Serve warm or cold with salad and mustard or mayonnaise.

## Cook's tips

• Plain pork sausagemeat is fine, as long as it is good quality, but often it is best to buy sausages and skin them, for better quality meat.
• You'll find it easier to mould the meat around the egg if your hands are wet, not floured

| | |
|---|---|
| Preparation time | 30 minutes |
| Cooking time | 45 minutes |
| Calories per egg | 381 Kcal |
| Fat per egg | 28g |
| of which saturated | 9.9g |
| Makes | 6 |

# Birmingham bacon cakes

These Brummy 'cakes' were served at country fairs in late Victorian times. They make a great brunch snack served warm, split and buttered on their own, or topped with scrambled egg and served with rocket and tomato salad.

**Streaky bacon** 5 rashers, de-rinded
**Self-raising flour** 225g (8oz)
**Butter** 25g (1oz)
**Mature Cheddar cheese** 75g (3oz), grated
**Salt and freshly ground black pepper**
**Milk** 150ml (¼ pint), plus a little for glazing
**Tomato ketchup** 1 tbsp
**Worcestershire sauce** 1 tsp

1 Preheat the oven to 200°C/400°F/Gas 6 and grease a baking sheet. Grill or dry fry the bacon until crisp, drain on kitchen paper and then crumble or chop it into small pieces.

2 Put the flour into a mixing bowl. Rub in the butter then add the bacon, half the grated cheese and some seasoning.

3 In a separate bowl, whisk the milk with the ketchup and Worcestershire sauce and add to the dry ingredients to make a soft dough.

4 On a lightly floured surface, knead the dough gently to a round then press it out with your hand to a circle about 18cm (7in) diameter. Place on the baking sheet and score into eight wedges.

5 Brush a little milk over the top (just use your finger). Sprinkle with the rest of the cheese.

6 Bake in the centre of the oven for 20–25 minutes. Transfer to a wire rack and serve warm or cool.

## Cook's tips

• Surprisingly for a scone-type mixture this 'cake' is fine to eat the next day, if kept wrapped in foil.
• A bacon cake is a good recipe to make if you suddenly realise that you have run out of bread!

| | |
|---|---|
| Preparation time | 15 minutes |
| Cooking time | 25 minutes |
| Calories per portion (4 servings) | 365 Kcal |
| Fat per portion (4 servings) | 15g |
| of which saturated | 8.5g |
| Serves | 4 as main course, 8 as accompaniment |

49

# Cornish pasties

Over the years, the pasty has become synonymous with Cornwall. It was a popular Cornish miner's lunch with meat and potato at one end and jam or fruit at the other. This recipe for mini, savoury pasties is ideal for a light lunch or snack.

**Potato** 1, peeled and very finely diced

**Carrot** 1, peeled and very finely diced

**Small onion** 1, peeled and very finely diced

**Lean beef steak** 225g (8oz), trimmed and cut into small pieces

**Salt and freshly ground black pepper**

**Shortcrust pastry** 450g (1lb)

**Egg** 1, beaten

## Cook's tips

• The finer you chop the filling ingredients, the more evenly the pasties will cook. You could grate the vegetables and mince the meat in a food processor or blender for convenience, but this would be less authentic.

• To freeze, allow to cool and then open freeze on trays or boards. Pack in a freezer bag or freezer-proof container and return to the freezer for up to three months. Allow to defrost in a refrigerator overnight and serve cold. To reheat, place in a preheated oven at 190°C/375°F/Gas 5 for about 20 minutes until piping hot.

| | |
|---|---|
| Preparation time | 30 minutes |
| Cooking time | 25 minutes |
| Calories per pasty | 630 Kcal |
| Fat per pasty | 140g |
| of which saturated | 16.8g |
| Makes | 4 |
| Suitable for freezing | |

1 Preheat the oven to 220°C/425°F/Gas 7. Mix together the potato, carrot, onion and steak and season well.

2 Roll out the pastry thinly on a lightly floured surface. Cut three saucer-sized circles, then use the trimmings to make a fourth. Divide the meat and vegetables between each circle, and brush the edges with egg.

3 Bring up the edges of each pasty to meet at the top. Crimp together the edges by pinching gently with the finger and thumb to seal.

4 Place on a baking sheet and brush all over with beaten egg. Bake for 10 minutes, then reduce the heat to 180°C/350°F/Gas 4 and cook for a further 15–20 minutes until golden and cooked through. Allow to cool for 10 minutes before serving with cherry tomatoes.

# Yorkshire roast beef salad

This unusual-sounding starter is a 21st-century take on the traditional Sunday dinner: roast beef with Yorkshire pudding. Originally, a large pudding was placed under a spit-roasted beef joint to catch all the juices. It was cut into pieces and served with the carved beef.

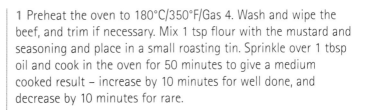

**Small lean beef joint,** such as fillet or topside 600g (1lb 5oz)

**Plain flour** 75g (3oz) plus 1 tsp

**English mustard powder** 1 tsp

**Salt and freshly ground black pepper**

**Sunflower oil** 2 tbsp

**Egg** 1

**Milk** 200ml (7fl oz)

**Reduced fat crème fraîche** 3 tbsp

**Creamed horseradish sauce** 1 tbsp

**Cooked beetroot in natural juice** 200g pack

**Watercress** 1 bunch

**Chopped parsley** 2 tbsp

**Asparagus tips** 110g (4oz), halved and blanched in boiling water for 3–4 minutes, to serve, optional

1 Preheat the oven to 180°C/350°F/Gas 4. Wash and wipe the beef, and trim if necessary. Mix 1 tsp flour with the mustard and seasoning and place in a small roasting tin. Sprinkle over 1 tbsp oil and cook in the oven for 50 minutes to give a medium cooked result – increase by 10 minutes for well done, and decrease by 10 minutes for rare.

2 Meanwhile, sift the remaining flour with a pinch of salt into a bowl. Make a well in the centre, add the egg and a quarter of the milk. Gently mix the flour into the liquid. Gradually whisk in the remaining milk to form a smooth batter. Transfer to a jug and let stand for 30 minutes.

3 When the beef is cooked, remove from the oven, cover loosely with foil and set aside. Raise the oven temperature to 220°C/425°F/Gas 7, divide the remaining oil between four 10cm (4in) diameter Yorkshire pudding tins and place in the oven for about 2 minutes until very hot. Remove from the oven, stir the batter and divide between the tins. Bake in the oven for about 25 minutes until well risen and golden. Remove from the tins and keep warm.

4 Just before serving, gently mix together the crème fraîche and horseradish sauce, cover and chill until required, drain the beetroot, reserving the juices, and cut into thin strips. Place the beetroot in a saucepan with the reserved juices and heat gently for 3–4 minutes until hot.

5 To serve, cut the beef into thin slices. Put each Yorkshire pudding into a bowl and top with slices of beef and hot beetroot, asparagus and watercress tossed in crème fraîche and horseradish and serve.

## Cook's tips

• The secret of a super light batter is not to over-beat it – over-mixing will make the puddings chewy.

• Avoid pickled cooked beetroot in this recipe as the flavour will be too strong.

| | |
|---|---|
| Preparation time | 15 minutes plus 30 minutes standing |
| Cooking time | 1 hour 30 minutes |
| Calories per portion | 409 Kcal |
| Fat per portion | 19g |
| of which saturated | 6.1g |
| Serves | 4 |

# Afternoon teas

Biscuits, bread, buns, doughnuts, gingerbread, pikelets, scones, shortbread and teacakes:  the list reads like an A–Z of comfort food. All are represented here, accompanied by cream, fruit, chocolate and syrup, and, more unexpectedly perhaps, by whisky, cider, saffron and pepper.

AFTERNOON TEAS

# Sumptuous sandwiches

Afternoon tea served in the garden on a summer's day is a quintessentially British occasion. The 'sandwich' acquired its name from the 4th Earl of Sandwich, who, it is said, introduced his 'rough and ready' sandwich into polite society – only to see it refined somewhat!

## Smoked salmon pin wheels

**Butter** 50g (2oz), softened
**Lemon** 1, finely zested rind and juice of half
**Watercress** 110g (4oz), chopped
**White or brown bread** 5 slices, crusts removed
**Smoked salmon** 200g packet, minimum 5 slices
**Freshly ground black pepper**

1 In a small bowl, mix together the butter, lemon rind and watercress. With a rolling pin, roll each slice of bread until it is about 3mm (⅛in) thick. Cut five sheets of greaseproof or non-stick baking paper, a little larger than the bread, then dampen with cold water – shaking off the excess.

2 Spread the slices of bread right up to the edges with the watercress butter, and then place each one on a sheet of the damp paper.

3 Cover the butter with the smoked salmon slices, trimming them to fit. Sprinkle with lemon juice, season with pepper and then, with the aid of the paper, roll up the bread and salmon together.

4 Wrap the rolls in the paper and twist the ends to seal, then chill well in the refrigerator for 1–2 hours, or overnight. Just before serving, cut the salmon rolls into slices, diagonally, approximately 1.5cm (½in) thick.

## Cucumber sandwiches

**Cucumber** ½ large (about 225g/8oz)
**Butter** 75g (3oz)
**Finely shredded mint** 2 tbsp
**Salt and freshly ground black pepper**
**White or brown bread** 6 slices

1 With a vegetable peeler, remove the skin from the cucumber, and then cut it into very thin slices, using the oblong cutting blade on a grater, or with a knife. Place the sliced cumber in a bowl, sprinkle with ½ tsp salt, cover and leave to stand for 10–15 minutes.

2 Blend together the butter and mint and season well with pepper.

3 Transfer the salted cucumber to a sieve, rinse under cold running water, and then drain well on kitchen paper.

4 Spread each slice of bread with the mint butter. Arrange the drained cucumber on half of the slices and then cover with the rest. Stack the sandwiches, wrap in cling film and refrigerate for 1–2 hours.

5 To serve, remove the crusts from the sandwiches and then cut into triangles, squares or oblongs as wished.

## Curried egg mayonnaise sandwiches

**Eggs** 3 large, hard-boiled and shelled
**Mayonnaise** 3 rounded tbsp
**Curry paste, medium or hot** 1–2 tsp
**White or brown bread** 6–8 thin slices
**Mustard and cress** 1 punnet

1 On a board, finely chop the eggs and then place them in a bowl. Add the mayonnaise and curry paste and mix together well.

2 Spread half of the bread with the egg mixture, add the mustard and cress, and then cover with the remaining slices of bread. Stack the sandwiches, wrap in cling film and refrigerate for 1–2 hours.

3 To serve, remove the crusts from the sandwiches and cut into triangles, squares or fingers as wished.

## Crab mayonnaise sandwiches

**Crabmeat** 175g (6oz)
**Mayonnaise** 1-2 tbsp
**Root ginger** 1–2 tsp, finely grated
**Freshly ground black pepper**
**White or brown bread** 8 slices
**Butter** 50g (2oz), softened
**Crisp lettuce leaves** 4–6

1 Place the crabmeat in a bowl and remove any pieces of shell, if necessary. Add the mayonnaise and ginger, season with pepper and mix well.

2 Spread each slice of bread with butter, and then spread half of the slices with the crabmeat and cover with the lettuce.

3 Cover the lettuce with the remaining slices and press well together. Stack the sandwiches, wrap in cling film and refrigerate for 1–2 hours.

4 To serve, remove the crusts from the sandwiches and then cut into quarters diagonally, or cut into three to make oblongs.

## Cream cheese and prawn sandwiches

**Fresh or frozen prawns** 175g (6oz), thawed and drained
**Cream cheese** 150g (5oz)
**Finely snipped chives** 3 tbsp
**Lemon juice** 1 tbsp
**Freshly ground black pepper**
**Brown or white bread** 8 thin slices
**Butter** 50g (2oz), softened
**Crisp lettuce leaves** 3–4, finely shredded

1 Finely chop the prawns and mix with the cream cheese, chives and lemon juice. Season with pepper.

2 Very thinly spread the bread with butter, and then spread half of the slices with the prawn mixture. Cover with the shredded lettuce, and then cover with the remaining bread. Stack the sandwiches, wrap in cling film and refrigerate for 1–2 hours.

3 To serve, remove the crusts from the sandwiches, and then cut into quarters diagonally or into four squares. Or, cut in half and then cut each half into fingers.

# Traditional homemade bread

Although wheat is grown in many parts of Britain, East Anglia and Lincolnshire are the largest producers. East Anglia also boasts a working water mill at Houghton in Cambridgeshire, which still makes wholemeal flour.

**Wholemeal bread**

**Warm water** 450ml (16fl oz)

**Caster sugar** 4 tsp

**Traditional dried active yeast** 1 tbsp

**Wholemeal flour** 680g (1½lb), plus a little extra for sifting

**Salt** 2 tsp

**Butter** 50g (2oz)

**Milk** 300ml (½ pint), warm

**Egg** 1 large beaten with 2 tbsp milk

**Oats** for sifting, optional

**White bread**

**Warm water** 150ml (¼ pint)

**Caster sugar** 4 tsp

**Traditional dried active yeast** 1 tbsp

**Organic strong plain flour** 680g (1½lb)

**Salt** 2 tsp

**Butter** 50g (2oz)

**Milk** 300ml (½ pint), warm

**Egg** 1 large beaten with 2 tbsp milk

**Oats** for sifting, optional

1 Place 150ml (¼ pint) of the warm water in a bowl or jug, add 1 tsp of the sugar and the yeast. Whisk well, then cover with cling film and leave to stand in a warm place for 15 minutes until a 5cm (2in) froth forms.

2 Meanwhile, sift the flour, remaining sugar and salt into a bowl, rub in the butter and make a well.

3 Whisk the yeast mixture and add to the flour, along with the remaining water and milk. Mix to a dough, then turn out onto a floured surface and knead until smooth and very elastic. Or mix with a dough hook in an electric mixer.

4 Cut the dough into 18 equally sized pieces and shape each one into a smooth ball. Place the balls on greased and lightly floured baking trays – well spaced apart. Loosely cover with cling film and leave to rise until doubled in size and retains an impression when lightly pressed with the tip of a finger – about 30 minutes.

5 To bake, preheat the oven to 230°C/450°F/Gas 8. The risen rolls may be sifted with flour and oats before baking, or brushed with milk or milk and beaten egg. Bake for 10–15 minutes until well risen, golden brown and sound hollow when tapped on the base. Cool on a wire rack.

## Cook's tip

• The ideal temperature for the warm water is 'blood heat', which is when the water feels neither hot nor cold when a finger is dipped into it.

| | |
|---|---|
| Preparation time | 10 minutes plus soaking and proving time |
| Cooking time | 15 minutes |
| Calories per roll | 144 Kcal |
| Fat per roll | 3g |
| of which saturated | 1.6g |
| Makes | 18 rolls |
| | Suitable for vegetarians |
| | Suitable for freezing |

# Scottish oatcakes

The climate in Scotland is perfect for oat growing, which means that oats and oatmeal feature in many of the national dishes. Scottish oatcakes are excellent with cheese so why not try making your own. They are very simple to create.

**Medium oatmeal** 110g (4oz) plus extra
**Salt** ¼ tsp
**Bicarbonate of soda** ¼ tsp
**Lard** 25g (1oz)
**Boiling water** 2–3 tbsp

1 Preheat the oven to 180°C/350°F/Gas 4 and grease a baking sheet. Put the oatmeal, salt and bicarbonate of soda into a bowl.

2 In a small saucepan, gently heat the lard until it has melted. Quickly pour enough of the liquid into the dry ingredients with the water to make a smooth dough.

3 Sprinkle some oatmeal onto a surface and roll out the dough to about 3mm (⅛in) thick. Then, using a 7.5cm (3in) round cutter, cut out 12 rounds, re-rolling the dough if necessary.

4 Place on the baking sheet and cook in the oven for around 20 minutes, until crisp. Serve lightly buttered with cheese, jam or Scottish heather honey.

## Cook's tip

• If you can find fine oatmeal, then use this to make an oatcake with a less coarse texture.

| | |
|---|---|
| Preparation time | 20 minutes |
| Cooking time | 10 minutes |
| Calories per oatcake | 53 Kcal |
| Fat per oatcake | 2g |
| of which saturated | 0.7g |
| Makes | 12 |
| Suitable for freezing | |

# Lancashire cheese scones

These are delicious served for afternoon tea, split in half and buttered – especially if they have just come out of the oven and are still warm. For a special occasion, serve them with a herb butter or mild chutney.

**Self-raising flour** 250g (9oz)
**Baking powder** 1 tsp
**Mustard powder** ½ tsp
**Butter** 50g (2oz)
**Lancashire cheese** 110g (4oz), grated
**Egg** 1
**Milk** 125ml (4fl oz), plus extra for glaze

1 Preheat the oven to 220°C/425°F/Gas 7. Butter a baking sheet.

2 Sift the flour, baking powder and mustard into a bowl. Add the butter and then rub it in until the mixture resembles fine breadcrumbs. Stir in 75g (3oz) of the cheese. Lightly beat the egg into the milk and then pour into the flour mixture. Use a round-bladed knife to bind together the ingredients. Knead the mixture very lightly to give a smooth surface.

3 Roll out the dough to 2cm (½in thick) and cut out rounds using a 6.5cm (2½in) round cutter and place them on the buttered baking sheet. Brush the tops of the scones with a little butter and then sprinkle over the remaining grated cheese.

4 Bake the scones towards the top of the oven for 12–15 minutes until they have risen and are a light golden colour. Remove from the oven, transfer to a wire rack and leave to cool. Serve them warm or cold.

## Cook's tip

• The Lancashire cheese gives a delicate flavour to these scones. If you prefer a stronger cheese flavour, then use an equal quantity of a mature Cheddar cheese.

| | |
|---|---|
| Preparation time | 15 minutes |
| Cooking time | 15 minutes |
| Calories per scone | 148 Kcal |
| Fat per scone | 7.3g |
| of which saturated | 4.3g |
| Makes | 12 |
| Suitable for vegetarians | |
| Suitable for freezing | |

# Sally Lunns

The story is that Sally Lunn was a refugee who travelled from France to England during the 17th century and made a living by selling buns in Bath from her secret recipe. The buns are large and flattish and are cut in half and served with savoury or sweet fillings.

**Strong plain flour** 500g (1lb 2oz)
**Fast–acting dried yeast** 7g sachet
**Salt** 1 tsp
**Eggs** 2, lightly beaten
**Milk** 300ml (½ pint), warmed to blood heat
**Butter** 50g (2oz) melted

1 Tip the flour into a bowl and stir in the yeast and salt. Reserve about 1 tbsp beaten egg, then beat the rest with the milk and butter and pour into the flour mixture. Mix together well to give a soft dough. Knead the dough for about 10 minutes on a lightly floured surface until it is stretchy.

2 Preheat the oven to 220°C/425°F/Gas 7 and butter two 18cm (7in) sandwich tins.

3 Divide the dough in half and shape each half into a flattish round ball and place in the sandwich tins. Cover with oiled cling film and leave them in a warm place until the dough has doubled in size.

4 Brush the reserved egg over the top of the loaves to glaze them. Bake the loaves towards the top of the oven for 15–20 minutes, until they have risen and are a golden colour. When lifted out of the tins, the loaves should sound hollow when tapped on the base – if they don't, return them to the oven and cook for a little longer.

5 Remove the loaves from the oven and transfer to a wire rack. Serve them warm or cold, split in half and served as they are or lightly toasted, or fill them with your favourite savoury combination and eat like a sandwich.

## Cook's tip

• If you want really glossy and deeper colour crusts, the buns may be brushed with a second coating of extra egg glaze halfway through the cooking process.

Preparation time – 15 minutes plus 30–45 minutes proving
Cooking time – 20 minutes
Calories per roll – 602 Kcal
Fat per roll – 17g
of which saturated – 8.4g
Serves – 4
Suitable for vegetarians

AFTERNOON TEAS

# Chestnut teacakes

The Romans are credited with bringing the sweet chestnut tree to Britain around 2000 years ago as their legions were fed on a diet that included flour made from chestnuts. Based on an early 19th-century recipe from Surrey, these teacakes can be served warm, cold or lightly toasted, spread with Cumberland rum butter (see opposite).

**Chestnuts** fresh 350g (12oz) or frozen 225g (8oz)

**Self-raising flour** 400g (14oz)

**Baking powder** 2 tsp

**Soft light brown sugar** 75g (3oz)

**Unsalted butter** 110g (4oz)

**Eggs** 2 large, beaten

**Milk** enough to make the beaten eggs up to 300ml (½ pint)

**Caster sugar** for sifting

1 If using fresh chestnuts, with a small, sharp knife cut a deep cross through the shell of each one, then place in a large saucepan, cover with cold water and bring to the boil. Reduce the heat and cook gently for 20 minutes – then remove from the heat. Using a slotted spoon, remove a few chestnuts at a time and carefully peel off the skins.

2 If using peeled, frozen chestnuts, place in a saucepan, cover with boiling water and cook gently for 6–8 minutes, or until tender – then drain well.

3 Pass the cooked chestnuts through a fine metal sieve, pressing them through with the back of a metal spoon. Allow the sieved nuts to cool.

4 Preheat the oven to 220°C/425°F/Gas 7.

5 Sift the flour, baking powder and sugar into a bowl. Mix in the sieved chestnuts and rub in the butter. Make a well in the centre. Slowly mix in the beaten eggs and milk until you have a soft, slightly sticky dough.

6 Turn the dough onto a floured surface and knead lightly until smooth – but do not over-knead.

7 Roll out the dough to approximately 2cm (¾in) thick. Using a well-floured 9cm (3½in) plain round cutter, stamp out rounds from the dough and place on a lightly floured baking sheet. Re-knead and re-roll the dough and cut out more rounds.

8 Brush the teacakes with a little milk (or use the egg and milk mixture from Step 5, if you have any left over), then bake for approximately 20 minutes, until well risen and lightly browned. They are cooked when they sound hollow when lightly tapped on the base.

9 Sift the hot teacakes with caster sugar then transfer to a wire rack to cool. Serve warm or cold, with or without butter.

## Cook's tip

• If you can't get hold of fresh or frozen whole chestnuts, use tinned or vacuum-packed chestnuts instead.

| | |
|---|---|
| Preparation time | 40 minutes |
| Cooking time | 20 minutes |
| Calories per teacake | 383 Kcal |
| Fat per teacake | 14g |
| of which saturated | 7.3g |
| Makes | 9 |
| Suitable for vegetarians | |

# Cumberland rum butter

Rum smuggling was once rife on the Cumbrian coastline, and rather than let 'accidentally broken' barrels of rum go to waste, the locals would take them home. Hence the creation of this butter, which is reputed to have been the creation of an elderly lady whose illegal cask of rum leaked all over the butter and brown sugar she had stored in her pantry.

**Unsalted butter** 175g (6oz), at room temperature
**Soft light brown sugar** 110g (4oz)
**Soft dark brown sugar** 110g (4oz)
**Grated nutmeg** 1 tsp
**Lemon juice** 2 tbsp
**Dark rum** 6 tbsp

1 Place the butter, both sugars, and nutmeg in a bowl and beat well with a hand-held electric mixer until very light and fluffy.

2 Whisk in the lemon juice, then very gradually whisk in the rum – whisking well between each addition. If added too fast the mixture will separate.

3 Spoon the butter into a ceramic or glass serving bowl – preferably one with a lid – and mark a swirl on the top with a small palette knife. Cover and refrigerate.

4 Serve the butter spread on warm crumpets or spooned on top of slices of hot, freshly baked apple pie. Due to the alcohol content of the butter, it can be spread straight from the refrigerator.

## Cook's tip

• Spread the rum butter the traditional way on slices of freshly baked gingerbread – but it is equally as good spread on warm scones, hot crumpets and toasted teacakes.

| | |
|---|---|
| Preparation time | 20 minutes |
| Calories per portion | 88 Kcal |
| Fat per portion | 5g |
| of which saturated | 3.4g |
| Serves | 27 |
| Suitable for vegetarians | |

# Buttery rowies

Buttery rowies are believed to have been made for Aberdeen fishermen who wanted bread that wouldn't go stale while they were on fishing trips. The 'rolls' are quite like croissants, and although their name implies they contain butter, they are made with vegetable fat.

**Strong plain flour** 450g (1lb)
**Salt** 1 tsp
**Caster sugar** 1 tbsp
**Fast acting dried yeast** 1½ tsp
**Luke warm water** 350ml (12fl oz)
**White vegetable fat** 350g (12oz), cut into small pieces

1 Sift the flour and salt into a mixing bowl and stir in the sugar and dried yeast. Make a well in the centre, stir in the water and mix well to form a medium soft dough. Cover loosely and place in a warm place for about an hour or until doubled in size.

2 Turn the dough onto a lightly floured surface and with a pressing/rolling action, form the dough into a long oblong measuring approximately 46 x 18cm (16 x 6in). This is quite difficult as the dough will be sticky. Dot one third of the white vegetable fat evenly all over the dough. Fold the top third of the dough down two thirds of the length, and then the bottom third up to cover the dough, giving a thick, even sided piece of square dough.

3 Turn the dough a quarter, and repeat the rolling process, adding half of the remaining fat, and then repeat the folding and turning. Roll out the dough once again, use up the remaining fat and fold up one more time. Roll and fold the dough two more times without adding fat.

4 Cut the dough into 16 equal-sized pieces and press/roll each one into a roughly square shape about 2cm (¾in thick). Transfer to greased and floured baking sheets and stand in a warm place for about 30 minutes until risen.

5 Preheat the oven to 200°C/400°F/Gas 6 and place a roasting tin half filled with boiling water in the bottom of the oven to create a steaming oven. Bake the rowies for 15 minutes until well risen, then remove the water and cook for a further 5 minutes until richly golden. They are best served warm, spread with butter, jam or marmalade.

## Cook's tips

• Rowies make a delicious alternative to a traditional bread roll and can be split and filled with any sweet or savoury fillings – they are also good split and toasted.
• To freeze, allow to cool, then place in a freezer bag or freezer-proof container. Freeze for up to three months. Re-heat from frozen on a baking tray at 180°C/ 350°F/Gas 4 for 10–15 minutes.

| | |
|---|---|
| Preparation time | 35 minutes plus 1½ hours proving time |
| Cooking time | 20 minutes |
| Calories per rowie | 296 Kcal |
| Fat per rowie | 22g |
| of which saturated | 4.8g |
| Makes | 16 |
| Suitable for vegetarians | |
| Suitable for freezing | |

# Bara pyglyd (pikelets)

The English name 'pikelet' is thought to be a corruption of the Welsh *bara pyglyd*. Traditionally, they would be cooked on a bake stone or griddle but here the cooking is done in a small frying pan for convenience.

**Strong plain flour** 450g (1lb)
**Salt** 1 tsp
**Caster sugar** 2 tsp
**Fast-acting dried yeast** 1 tbsp
**Milk** 600ml (1 pint), warmed
**Vegetable oil** 1 tbsp

**1** Sift the flour, salt and sugar into a bowl and stir in the yeast. Make a well in the centre and pour in the milk. Gradually mix into the dry ingredients to form a thick batter. Set aside in a warm place for about an hour until the batter is frothy and has doubled in size.

**2** Lightly brush a 15cm (6in) diameter frying pan with a little oil and heat until hot. Ladle in sufficient batter to a depth of 2cm (½in) and cook over a low/moderate heat for about 6 minutes until the bubbles on the surface burst and set.

**3** Carefully, slide a palette knife under the pikelet and turn it over and cook for a further 2 minutes until lightly golden. Transfer to a wire rack to cool, and continue to make pikelets until all the batter is used up – you should be able to make seven. They are best served warm with butter and jam.

## Cook's tips

• Fast-acting dried yeast is very easy and convenient to use, but unlike other forms of yeast it must be added to the dry ingredients first. If you mix it with liquid first, it is rendered inactive.
• To freeze, allow the pikelets to cool, then layer between sheets of baking parchment. Place the stack in a freezer bag, wrap well in foil or place in a freezer-proof container. Freeze for up to three months. Allow to thaw overnight in the refrigerator. To reheat, divide into two stacks and place on a baking sheet lined with baking parchment. Cover with foil and place in a preheated oven at 190°C/375°F/Gas 5 for about 8 minutes until piping hot.

| | |
|---|---|
| Preparation time | 15 minutes plus 1 hour proving time |
| Cooking time | 1 hour |
| Calories per pikelet | 282 Kcal |
| Fat per pikelet | 4g |
| of which saturated | 1.2g |
| Makes | 7 |
| Suitable for vegetarians | |
| Suitable for freezing | |

# Cornish splits

These yeasted buns may be served with jam and clotted cream as part of a Cream Tea in place of scones. When served with black treacle or golden syrup and clotted cream they are known as 'Thunder and Lightning'.

**Strong plain flour** 500g (1lb 2oz)
**Butter** 50g (2oz)
**Salt** 1 tsp
**Caster sugar** 1 tsp
**Fast-acting dried yeast** 7g sachet
**Milk** 300ml (½ pint), warmed
**Jam or syrup and clotted cream** to serve
**Icing sugar** to dust

1 Tip the flour into a bowl, add the butter and rub it in until the mixture resembles fine breadcrumbs. Stir in the salt, sugar and dried yeast and then add the warm milk and mix to bind the ingredients into a soft dough. Knead the dough on a lightly floured surface for 5–7 minutes until it's smooth and elastic.

2 Divide the dough into 12 and shape each into a round ball with a smooth surface and flatten them slightly. Place the balls on a buttered and floured baking sheet in three rows of four with about 2cm (½in) between them so that when they rise they will touch each other. Cover the baking tray with an oiled freezer bag or with a clean dry tea towel. Leave the splits in a warm place for 30–40 minutes or until they have doubled in size.

3 Preheat the oven to 220°C/425°F/Gas 7. Bake the splits in the centre of the oven for about 15 minutes or until they are a light golden colour and sound hollow when tapped underneath. Remove from the oven and transfer to a wire rack to cool. Serve the splits warm or cold, filled with jam or syrup and clotted cream and dusted with a little sifted icing sugar.

## Cook's tip

• It is important that you buy fast-acting dried yeast. The slow-acting variety, apart from taking longer, of course, is also a lot more tricky to use.

| | |
|---|---|
| Preparation time | 10 minutes plus 30–40 minutes proving |
| Cooking time | 15 minutes |
| Calories per split | 187 Kcal |
| Fat per split | 4g |
| of which saturated | 2.5g |
| Makes | 12 |
| Suitable for vegetarians | |
| Suitable for freezing | |

'For there's Bishop's teign
And King's teign
And Coomb at the clear Teign head –
Where close by the stream
You may have your cream
All spread upon barley bread.'
John Keats

# Maids of honour

These dainty afternoon teacakes were given their name by Henry VIII after he was offered a cake in the gardens of Hampton Court Palace by one of Catherine of Aragon's ladies, known as maids of honour. It is said that one of those maids was Anne Boleyn, who subsequently became his second queen.

**Shortcrust pastry** 500g packet
**Curd cheese** 227g tub
**Eggs** 2 large
**Soft light brown sugar** 110g (4oz)
**Single cream** 4 tbsp
**Brandy, orange flower water or rosewater** 2 tbsp
**Ground almonds** 150g (5oz)
**Seedless raisins** 50g (2oz), finely chopped
**Caster or icing sugar** for sifting

## Cook's tips

• Although these maids of honour are best eaten on the same day as baking, they can be stored in an airtight tin for two to three days and still taste good, even though the pastry does soften a little.
• You can also make them with ready-made puff pastry, using the same quantities and cooking time.

| | |
|---|---|
| Preparation time | 30 minutes |
| Cooking time | 15–20 minutes |
| Calories per cake | 177 Kcal |
| Fat per cake | 11g |
| of which saturated | 3.4g |
| Makes | 24 |
| Suitable for vegetarians | |

1 Preheat the oven to 220°C/425°F/Gas 7. Roll the pastry out very thinly – just a little thinner than a one penny piece. Using an 8.5cm (3¼in) fluted or plain round cutter, stamp out 24 rounds from the pastry, re-folding and re-rolling the trimmings if necessary.

2 Line two deep-hole bun tin trays (each hole approximately 6.5cm wide/2cm deep) with the pastry rounds. Chill while making the filling.

3 Place the curd cheese, eggs, sugar, cream, brandy or flower water and almonds in a mixing bowl and beat well together with a whisk. Mix in the raisins and then spoon into the pastry cases.

4 Bake the tarts for 15–20 minutes until well risen, golden brown and feel firm to the touch. Allow the maids of honour to cool a little and then carefully remove them onto a wire rack to cool completely. Sift with icing or caster sugar and serve.

# Singin' hinnies

'Hinny' is a corruption of honey, a Tyneside term of endearment referring to children and young women. These 'hinnies' are cooked on a grid iron and got their name from the 'singing' sound they make as they cook. In the 19th century, silver threepenny pieces were inserted in the cakes, especially for the children at birthday parties.

**Plain flour** 250g (8oz)
**Bicarbonate of soda** ⅛ tsp
**Cream of tartar** ¼ tsp
**Salt** ¼ tsp
**Butter** 75g (3oz)
**Sultanas** 75g (3oz)
**Milk** 7 tbsp

1 Sift the flour, bicarbonate of soda, cream of tartar and salt into a large bowl. Rub in the butter then add the sultanas. Mix in enough milk to give a soft dough.

2 Put a griddle pan or heavy-based frying pan on a low heat to heat up. Roll out the dough on a lightly floured surface to only just over 5mm (¼in) thick. Cut out 7cm (2¾in) rounds, re-rolling the trimmings to make more cakes.

3 Lightly butter the griddle or pan and cook the rounds for 4 minutes until patched brown underneath then turn and cook for another 4 minutes. You may need to do this in two batches if your pan is small. Serve hot with butter, jam or clotted cream.

## Cook's tips

• Don't be tempted to turn the cakes too soon or they may be 'doughy' in the middle.
• Some recipes use currants or raisins or a mixture of fruits and some add a little sugar and even cream, so there are probably not just regional differences but family recipes passed down the generations.

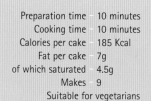

| | |
|---|---|
| Preparation time | 10 minutes |
| Cooking time | 10 minutes |
| Calories per cake | 185 Kcal |
| Fat per cake | 7g |
| of which saturated | 4.5g |
| Makes | 9 |
| Suitable for vegetarians | |

# Isle of Wight doughnuts

Associations with the island and these fruited doughnuts can be traced back to the mid-19th century, and they are well documented as part of Shrove Tuesday traditions, when locals used up all the rich storecupboard ingredients before the Lenten fasting began.

**Strong plain flour** 175g (6oz)
**Plain flour** 175g (6oz)
**Salt** ½ tsp
**Unsalted butter** 50g (2oz)
**Caster sugar** 50g (2oz) plus extra for sifting
**Ground nutmeg** ¼ tsp
**Fast-acting dried yeast** 2 tsp
**Milk** 175ml (6fl oz), luke warm
**Currants** 50g (2oz)
**Mixed candied peel** 50g (2oz), chopped
**Vegetable oil** for deep frying

1 Sift the flours and salt into a mixing bowl and rub in the butter until the mixture resembles breadcrumbs. Stir in the sugar and then the nutmeg and yeast. Make a well in the centre and gradually blend in the milk to form a soft dough. Cover loosely, stand in a warm place for about an hour or until doubled in size.

2 Mix together the currants and peel and set aside.

3 Turn the dough onto a lightly floured surface and knead until smooth. Divide into 12 equal portions. Flatten each piece and place a little of the dried fruit in the centre. Gather the edges together over the filling, pinch to seal and roll into a ball. Set aside on a lightly greased tray while heating the oil.

4 Heat the oil for deep frying in a large saucepan to 160°C (315°F) and cook the doughnuts in two batches for about 10 minutes, turning halfway through, until they are puffy and golden. Drain well and sift over extra caster sugar. The doughnuts are best served warm.

## Cook's tips

• For jam doughnuts, omit the nutmeg and dried fruit. Replace the filling with 1 tsp strawberry jam per dough round. Cook as above. Make sure you seal the dough very well to avoid the filling spilling out during cooking.
• To freeze, omit sifting with sugar. Allow the doughnuts to cool, open freeze on trays or boards and pack in a freezer bag or freezer-proof container for up to three months. Allow to defrost at room temperature and sift with sugar before serving.

| | |
|---|---|
| Preparation time | 25 minutes plus 1 hour proving time |
| Cooking time | 20 minutes |
| Calories per doughnut | 270 Kcal |
| Fat per doughnut | 15g |
| of which saturated | 3.6g |
| Makes | 12 |
| | Suitable for vegetarians |
| | Suitable for freezing |

# Cornish fairings

With their brown crackled top, these biscuits have been made since the 1880s for fairs and markets in Cornwall, then in the West Country and now the whole nation. Fairings were often bought as a sweet treat for a girlfriend.

**Plain flour** 110g (4oz)
**Salt** ¼ tsp
**Baking powder** 1 tsp
**Bicarbonate of soda** 1 tsp
**Ground ginger** 1 tsp
**Ground cinnamon** 1 tsp
**Mixed spice** 1 tsp
**Butter** 50g (2oz)
**Granulated sugar** 50g (2oz)
**Lemon** 1, finely grated rind only
**Golden syrup** 2 tbsp

1 Preheat the oven to 200°C/400°F/Gas 6 and butter two baking sheets.

2 Sift the flour, salt, baking powder, bicarbonate of soda and spices into a bowl. Rub in the butter and then stir in the sugar and lemon rind. Warm the syrup and measure out the 2 tbsp. Stir into the mixture to make a dough that should stick together but not be sticky.

3 Roll half the mixture into walnut-sized balls (about 7g /¼oz) each and place on a baking sheet, leaving room for them to spread. Bake on the top shelf of the oven. When they begin to colour – check after 5 and then 6 minutes – put them on the lower shelf for 1–2 minutes where they will 'flop and crack' to the familiar fairing.

4 Repeat with the rest of the mixture. Cool the biscuits on a wire rack.

## Cook's tips

• After the first batch you'll know how long to leave them on the bottom shelf so that they crisp but do not burn.
• The biscuits will keep in an airtight tin for a week.

| | |
|---|---|
| Preparation time | 20 minutes |
| Cooking time | 15 minutes |
| Calories per fairing | 72 Kcal |
| Fat per fairing | 2.7g |
| of which saturated | 1.7g |
| Makes | 15 |
| Suitable for vegetarians | |
| Suitable for freezing | |

**69**

# Brighton rock cakes

These craggy cakes are meant to look like rocks and the mixture needs to be quite dry to give the rough appearance. Don't be tempted to add any liquid or the buns will spread out.

**Self-raising flour** 250g (9oz)
**Butter** 75g (3oz)
**Dried mixed fruit** 75g (3oz)
**Caster sugar** 75g (3oz), plus extra for sprinkling
**Egg** 1
**Salt** pinch

## Cook's tip

• Any dried fruits may be used. For example, dried apricots with a little ground cinnamon works well.

| | |
|---|---|
| Preparation time | 10 minutes |
| Cooking time | 15 minutes |
| Calories per cake | 164 Kcal |
| Fat per cake | 6g |
| of which saturated | 3.4g |
| Makes | 12 |
| Suitable for vegetarians | |
| Suitable for freezing | |

1 Preheat the oven to 190°C/375°F/Gas 5 and butter a baking sheet.

2 Sift the flour into a bowl. Cut the butter into pieces and then rub it into the flour. Stir in the fruit, sugar, egg and salt. Use a fork to work the mixture together into a stiff dough. Divide the mixture into 12 roughly shaped balls and place them on the buttered baking sheet. Roughen the surface of the cakes with a fork. Sprinkle a little extra caster sugar over the cakes.

3 Bake the cakes in the centre of the oven for 12–15 minutes until they are a light golden colour. Remove from the oven and transfer to a wire rack and leave to cool. Store the cakes in an airtight container for up to three days.

# Brandy snaps

These are often sold at fairs in the Midlands, either flat or curled. Make them today as tuilles to serve with ice cream or cream and fruit.

**Caster sugar** 50g (2oz)
**Butter** 50g (2oz)
**Golden syrup** 50g (2oz)
**Plain flour** 50g (2oz)
**Salt** pinch
**Ground ginger** 1 tsp
**Brandy** 1 tsp
**Lemon juice** ½ tsp

1 Preheat the oven to 200°C/400°F/Gas 6. Line two baking sheets with greaseproof paper and have a long rolling pin ready for curling the biscuits over and a cooling rack.

2 Put the sugar, butter and syrup in a small pan and stir over a low heat until the sugar melts and the mixture blends together. Don't let the mixture get too hot. Take the pan off the heat and add the rest of the ingredients. Beat well until smooth.

3 Cook the biscuits in batches. Put 6 tsp of the mixture spaced apart on one baking sheet. Bake for 5 minutes then check the colour. They should be lacy and golden brown. Put them back in for another couple of minutes but watch they do not 'catch' round the edges.

4 Take them out, put the second baking sheet with another 6 tsp of the mixture on in the oven. Let the first batch cool for about half a minute then quickly ease them off the tray with a palette knife and drape over a rolling pin so that as they set, they will form a tuille shape. It only takes a minute for them to set. Continue with the production line until all the mixture is used. Fill with fruit or cream and serve immediately.

## Cook's tips

• Measure the flour out first, then you won't have to wash the scale pan.
• Warm the syrup for measuring it and do this after the butter as then the syrup will be easier to scrape off the scale pan.
• Store the biscuits in an airtight tin. If they are left out in a steamy kitchen, they may soften. They are also best eaten on the day or the day after making.
• Keep the biscuits flat if you prefer or roll them round thick wooden spoon handles for brandy snap rolls. Work quickly otherwise they will snap!

| | |
|---|---|
| Preparation time | 10 minutes |
| Cooking time | 6–7 minutes per batch |
| Calories per snap | 38 Kcal |
| Fat per snap | 2g |
| of which saturated | 1.1g |
| Makes | 24 |
| Suitable for vegetarians | |
| Suitable for freezing | |

# Fat rascals

There is lots of history behind these biscuits, and they may originally have been cooked on open turf or peat fires on Whitby Moor. Another suggestion is that they were made from trimmings of shortcrust pastry that were rolled out and had currants and sugar sprinkled over the top. They were then baked and eaten warm, with butter spread over them.

**Plain flour** 250g (9oz)
**Salt** pinch
**Butter** 110g (4oz)
**Currants** 50g (2oz)
**Light muscovado sugar** 2 tbsp
**Milk** 3–4 tbsp
**Caster sugar** for sprinkling

1 Preheat the oven to 200°C/400°F/Gas 6. Butter a baking sheet.

2 Sift the flour into a bowl and add the salt. Rub in the butter, then stir in the currants and sugar. Add the milk and bind to form a dough. Knead the dough lightly on a floured surface and then roll it out to about 1cm (½in) thick.

3 Use a 5cm (2in) cutter to cut out rounds and place them on the baking sheet. Re-roll and cut trimmings as necessary. Sprinkle caster sugar over the tops. Cook in the centre of the oven for 15–18 minutes. These will keep in an airtight container for up to three days.

## Cook's tip

• Some people make these into faces by arranging currants for the eyes and nose and flaked almonds for the teeth.

| | |
|---|---|
| Preparation time | 10 minutes |
| Cooking time | 18 minutes |
| Calories per biscuit | 200 Kcal |
| Fat per biscuit | 9g |
| of which saturated | 5.8g |
| Makes | 10 |
| Suitable for vegetarians | |

# Almond shortbread

Years ago it was traditional to break a piece of shortbread over a bride's head as she crossed the threshold of her new home, but today Scottish shortbread has become an essential component of afternoon tea nationwide. In Scotland it is far more likely to be served for high tea – a late afternoon/early evening meal created by the Scots.

**Plain flour** 200g (7oz)

**Salt** pinch

**Ground almonds** 50g (2oz)

**Caster sugar** 50g (2oz), plus extra for sifting

**Unsalted butter** 250g (9oz)

**Whole almonds** 50g (2oz), blanched and skinned, to decorate, optional

**Glacé cherries** 10

1 Preheat the oven to 150°C/300°F/Gas 2. Sift the flour and salt into a mixing bowl. Add the ground almonds and caster sugar and mix well.

2 Rub the butter into the flour and sugar until the mixture forms coarse crumbs, then gently work the mixture together until it forms a ball.

3 Lightly knead the dough on a floured surface until smooth, then roll out into a neat round a little smaller than a 25cm (10in) fluted, loose-bottom flan tin.

4 Place the shortbread in the tin and press out gently into the flutes. Smooth the surface with the back of a tablespoon.

5 Arrange the blanched almonds and cherries on top of the shortbread, lightly pressing them into the surface.

6 Bake the shortbread in the centre of the oven for 30–35 minutes, until very lightly browned. Remove the shortbread from the oven, sift caster sugar lightly over the surface and then allow it to cool in the tin. When cold, cut the shortbread into wedges for serving. Store in an airtight tin.

## Cook's tips

• You will find it easier to rub the butter in if it is used chilled.

• If you do not have a loose-bottom tin, line the base of the tin with baking parchment.

| | |
|---|---|
| Preparation time | 20 minutes |
| Cooking time | 35 minutes |
| Calories per triangle | 390 Kcal |
| Fat per triangle | 28g |
| of which saturated | 13g |
| Makes | 10 shortbread triangles |
| Suitable for vegetarians | |

# Grantham gingerbreads

In the 1740s, a baker in Grantham, Lincolnshire, was making Grantham whetstones – a hard flat biscuit, offered to travellers for their journey. The story goes that he got the recipe wrong, and that's how Grantham gingerbreads were invented!

**Butter** 100g (3½oz), softened
**Caster sugar** 250g (9oz)
**Egg** 1
**Self-raising flour** 250g (9oz)
**Ground ginger** 1 tsp

1 Preheat the oven to150°C/300°F/Gas 2. Cream together the butter and sugar until light and fluffy and then beat in the egg. Sift in the flour and ginger.

2 Mix well to bind the mixture together and form into small balls – 1 tbsp of mixture per ball. Place spaced apart on two or three non-stick or lightly greased baking sheets as they spread while cooking.

3 Bake for 25–35 minutes (in batches if necessary) until just lightly browned. Leave on the baking sheet for a minute and then cool on a wire rack.

'I think I've sipp'd my tea nigh up,
O! yes, I'm sure I drank my cup;
I work till supper, after that
I play or sing, or maybe chat;
At ten we always go to bed,
And thus my life I've calmly led.'

Susanna Blamire

## Cook's tip

• These biscuits keep well in an airtight tin for a week.

| | |
|---|---|
| Preparation time | 20 minutes |
| Cooking time | 25–30 mins per batch |
| Calories per biscuit | 89 Kcal |
| Fat per biscuit | 25g |
| of which saturated | 1.8g |
| Makes | 30 biscuits |
| Suitable for vegetarians | |
| Suitable for freezing | |

# Bara brith

*Bara brith* means 'speckled bread'. This recipe evolved as a way to use up leftover dough and incorporate ingredients in the storecupboard. It is traditionally served as a snack or sweet treat in a lunchbox, but is equally good spread with butter and served with tea.

**Strong plain flour** 450g (1lb)
**Salt** 1 tsp
**Mixed spice** 1½ tsp
**Caster sugar** 4 tbsp
**Currants** 225g (8oz)
**Mixed candied peel** 50g (2oz)
**Fast-acting dried yeast** 1½ tsp
**Skimmed milk** 225ml (8fl oz), luke warm
**Unsalted butter** 50g (2oz), melted
**Eggs** 1 large, beaten, and 1 small, beaten, to glaze

## Cook's tips

• Try toasting slices of bara brith and serving at breakfast time, spread with marmalade.
• To freeze, allow the loaf to cool, then slice. Layer the slices between sheets of baking parchment and place in a freezer bag. Seal well and freeze for up to three months. Thaw a few slices at a time.

| | |
|---|---|
| Preparation time | 20 minutes plus 1½ hours proving time |
| Cooking time | 40 minutes |
| Calories per slice | 174 Kcal |
| Fat per slice | 3g |
| of which saturated | 1.7g |
| Makes | 1 loaf (18 slices) |
| Suitable for vegetarians | |
| Suitable for freezing | |

1 Sift the flour, salt and mixed spice into a mixing bowl and stir in the sugar, currants, peel and yeast. Make a well in the centre and gradually blend in the milk, butter and egg to form a soft dough.

2 Turn on to a lightly floured surface and knead for about 5 minutes until smooth and elastic. Place in a floured bowl, cover loosely and stand in a warm place for about an hour or until doubled in size.

3 Turn the dough onto a lightly floured surface and re-knead until smooth. Form the dough into a sausage shape and place in a lightly greased 900g (2lb) loaf tin. Stand in a warm place for a further 30 minutes or so until well risen.

4 Preheat the oven to 200°C/400°F/Gas 6. Brush the bread with beaten egg and bake for about 40 minutes until richly golden, crusty and risen (cover with foil if it starts browning too quickly) – the bread should sound hollow when tapped. Turn on to a wire rack to cool. It is best served sliced, spread with butter.

# Shrewsbury biscuits

Originally made in 1760 by a Mr Palin in Shropshire, these biscuits were bought as gifts by visitors in much the same way as shortbread in Scotland or clotted cream in Devon. They have a light texture and lemony flavour and are very simple to prepare.

**Butter** 110g (4oz)

**Caster sugar** 150g (5oz), plus extra for sprinkling

**Egg yolks** 2

**Plain flour** 225g (8oz)

**Lemon** 1, finely grated rind only

**Chopped dried fruit** 50g (2oz)

1 Preheat the oven to 180°C/350°F/Gas 4 and butter two non-stick baking sheets.

2 Cream the butter and sugar until pale and fluffy and add the egg yolks and beat well. Add the flour, lemon rind and fruit and mix to a fairly firm dough.

3 On a lightly floured surface, knead lightly and then roll out to about 5mm (¼in) thick. Cut out 6.5cm (2½in) rounds with a fluted cutter and place on the baking sheets. Sprinkle with a little extra caster sugar.

4 Bake for 12–15 minutes until lightly browned and firm to the touch. Transfer to wire racks to cool. Store in an airtight container.

## Cook's tip

• If you enjoy spiced biscuits, omit the lemon rind and add 1 tsp mixed spice and 1 tsp cinnamon instead.

| | |
|---|---|
| Preparation time | 30 minutes |
| Cooking time | 15 minutes |
| Calories per biscuit | 102 Kcal |
| Fat per biscuit | 4g |
| of which saturated | 2.9g |
| Makes | 24 biscuits |
| Suitable for vegetarians | |
| Suitable for freezing | |

AFTERNOON TEAS

# Malvern cherry cake

Malvern, in Worcestershire, is famous for its mineral water, for being the birthplace of Sir Edward Elgar and for this light Madeira-style cake. Serve it on a Royal Worcester plate if you have one!

**Glacé cherries** 200g tub
**Butter** 225g (8oz), softened
**Caster sugar** 225g (8oz)
**Eggs** 4 large
**Lemon** 1, finely grated rind and juice
**Self-raising flour** 350g (12oz)
**Milk** 3 tbsp
**Chopped mixed peel** 1 tbsp
**Icing sugar** for dusting, optional

1 Preheat the oven to 160°C/325°F/Gas 3 and grease and line a 20cm (8in) deep cake tin with greaseproof paper.

2 Rinse the cherries under warm water, dry them in a tea towel and cut them into quarters.

3 Cream together the butter and sugar until fluffy and then beat in the eggs, one at a time. Stir in the lemon rind and juice.

4 Toss the cherries in some of the flour. Fold in the rest of the flour, then stir in the cherries and milk. Spoon into the prepared tin and smooth the top, making a very slight dip in the middle. Sprinkle the mixed peel over the top and bake for 1 hour 20 minutes – checking occasionally after it has been in the oven an hour. The cake should be firm.

5 Take the cake out of the oven and leave to cool in the tin for about 15 minutes. Then turn onto a wire rack. Dust with icing sugar, if you like.

## Cook's tips

• The cake will keep in an airtight tin for a week.
• Traditionally the cake was decorated with candied lemon – in large or small pieces – and there were more cherries, all left whole.
• Cherries have an annoying tendency to gravitate towards the bottom of a cake. Washing, drying, chopping and dusting them in flour should help prevent that but don't worry if they are still near the base and don't apologise for it! It's a lovely light lemony cake – with a layer of cherries.

| | |
|---|---|
| Preparation time | 15 minutes |
| Cooking time | 1 hour 20 minutes |
| Calories per slice | 289 Kcal |
| Fat per slice | 14g |
| of which saturated | 7.8g |
| Serving | 1 cake (16 slices) |
| Suitable for vegetarians | |
| Suitable for freezing | |

# Cider cake

The West Country is synonymous with apples and Cider production. In fact, Glastonbury was called Avalon – 'The Isle of Apples' – by Iron Age people. The cider in this cake creates a moist texture and apple flavour.

**Dry cider** 150ml (¼ pint)
**Sultanas** 225g (8oz)
**Butter** 110g (4oz)
**Light soft brown sugar** 110g (4oz)
**Eggs** 2, beaten
**Plain flour** 225g (8oz)
**Bicarbonate of soda** 1 tsp

## Cook's tip

• Don't leave this cake for too long in the oven because it will start to dry out and become very crumbly.

Preparation time – 10 minutes
Cooking time – 45–60 minutes
Calories per square – 179 Kcal
Fat per square – 7g
of which saturated – 3.9g
Makes – 16 squares
Suitable for vegetarians
Suitable for freezing

1 Put the cider and fruit in a bowl and leave to soak overnight.

2 Preheat the oven to 180°C/350°F/Gas 4, grease an 18cm (7in) square cake tin and line with baking parchment.

3 Cream the butter and sugar until pale and fluffy. Gradually add the eggs, beating well after each addition. Add half of the flour and all the bicarbonate of soda and mix well.

4 Add the cake mixture to the cider and sultanas and mix thoroughly. Fold in the remaining flour and then pour into the prepared tin.

5 Bake for 45–60 minutes, until well risen and firm to the touch. Leave to cool for 30 minutes before turning out onto a wire rack. Leave to cool completely and then cut into squares or slices.

# Courting cake

This attractive cake was originally baked by young ladies for their betrothed. It is a real summer treat. Bake it in August, when strawberries should be good value.

**Butter** 225g (8oz)
**Caster sugar** 225g (8oz)
**Eggs** 4, beaten
**Self-raising flour** 350g (12oz)
**Milk** 2–3 tbsp
**Double cream** 300ml (½ pint), whipped
**Strawberries** 225g (8oz), sliced
**Icing sugar** for dusting

1 Preheat the oven 180°C/350°F/Gas 4 and grease and line three 18cm (7in) round sandwich cake tins.

2 Cream together the butter and sugar until pale and fluffy. Gradually add the eggs, beating well after each addition. Fold in the flour and then add enough milk to give a dropping consistency.

3 Divide the mixture between the three cake tins and bake in the oven for 25–30 minutes until well risen and firm. Turn out and leave to cool on a wire rack.

4 Whip the cream until it holds soft peaks. Sandwich together the cakes with the cream and strawberries, reserving a few for decoration. Dust the top with icing sugar and decorate with strawberries.

## Cook's tips

• If you only have two sandwich tins, follow the method using 175g (6oz) each of butter, sugar and flour, 3 eggs and 2 tbsp milk. Cook at 180°C/350°F/Gas 4 for 20–25 minutes.
• Decorate just before serving so the strawberry juices don't have time to run and discolour the cream.

| | |
|---|---|
| Preparation time | 10 minutes |
| Cooking time | 25 minutes |
| Calories per slice | 356 Kcal |
| Fat per slice | 24g |
| of which saturated | 13.5g |
| Makes | 16 slices |
| Suitable for vegetarians | |

'How sweet I roam'd from field to field,
And tasted all the summer's pride,
Till I the prince of love beheld,
Who in the sunny beams did glide!
He shew'd me lilies for my hair,
And blushing roses for my brow;
He led me through his gardens fair,
Where all his golden pleasures grow.'
William Blake

# Chocolate whisky cake

Every Scottish baker has their own recipe for chocolate cake and this one incorporates whisky, which complements the flavour of the chocolate. There is also a hidden ingredient (a Scottish favourite), which helps give the cake its rich, moist texture.

**Very dark plain chocolate** 175g (6oz)
**Unsalted butter** 110g (4oz), softened
**Light brown sugar** 175g (6oz)
**Cold finely mashed potato** 75g (3oz)
**Eggs** 2, beaten
**Self-raising flour** 175g (6oz)
**Salt** ½ tsp
**Milk** 4 tbsp
**Double cream** 125ml (4fl oz)
**Icing sugar** 50g (2oz), sifted
**Whisky** 3 tbsp
**Raspberry jam** 3 tbsp
**Raspberries** to decorate

## Cook's tips

• If whisky isn't your preferred tipple, dark rum or brandy also works well with chocolate, or replace with orange juice for a non-alcoholic version. If you have any cake left, it is best stored in a sealed container, but allow to stand at room temperature before serving.
• Freeze without icing and filling. Allow the sponges to cool and then wrap well in cling film and foil. Freeze for up to three months. Allow to cool at room temperature before filling and icing.

| | |
|---|---|
| Preparation time | 25 minutes |
| Cooking time | 25 minutes |
| Calories per portion | 435 Kcal |
| Fat per portion | 24g |
| of which saturated | 13.6g |
| Serving | 10 |
| Suitable for vegetarians | |
| Suitable for freezing | |

**1** Preheat the oven to 190°C/375°F/Gas 5 and grease and line two 20cm (8in) Victoria sandwich cake tins. In a heatproof bowl, break 50g (2oz) of the chocolate, and place over a pan of gently simmering water to melt.

**2** In another bowl, beat together the butter and brown sugar until pale. Beat in the melted chocolate and mashed potato.

**3** Gradually beat in the eggs, adding a little of the flour with each. Sift the remaining flour and salt into the mixture and add the milk. Gently fold together until well combined.

**4** Divide the mixture equally between the prepared tins and smooth over the tops. Bake for about 25 minutes until risen and springy-firm to the touch. Turn onto wire racks to cool completely.

**5** Melt the remaining chocolate as above and cool for 10 minutes. Add the cream, the icing sugar and the whisky. Carefully whisk together until thick and creamy. Spread the jam over one half of the cake and then spread half the chocolate cream on top. Sandwich together with the other half. Spread the remaining chocolate cream on top. Decorate with fresh raspberries before serving.

# Cornish saffron cake

It is understood that saffron was first brought to Britain by the Phoenicians, who traded the bright yellow powder for Cornish tin. This cake is like a bread and is cooked in a loaf tin. It's good served as plain slices or toast it and spread with butter.

**Saffron** large pinch dried strands
**Boiling water** 2 tbsp
**Strong plain flour** 450g (1lb)
**Butter** 75g (3oz)
**Lard** 40g (1½oz)
**Salt** large pinch
**Currants** 200g (7oz)
**Cut mixed peel** 50g (2oz)
**Caster sugar** 2 tbsp
**Fast-acting dried yeast** 7g sachet
**Eggs** 2
**Milk** 125ml (4fl oz), luke warm
**Almond essence** few drops

1 Butter a 900g (2lb) loaf tin. Place the saffron on a sheet of baking parchment and place it in a coolish oven for a few minutes to dry it out. Crumble into a small bowl and pour over 2 tbsp boiling water and leave it to steep for at least 1 hour.

2 Tip the flour into a bowl, and then rub in the butter and lard until the mixture resembles breadcrumbs. Stir in the salt, currants, peel, caster sugar and yeast.

3 Beat together the eggs, milk, almond essence and steeped saffron. Pour the liquid into the flour mixture and mix to form a soft dough. Turn out onto a lightly floured surface and knead it for about 10 minutes until it's smooth and elastic. Shape into a smooth loaf and place in the tin. Cover with a sheet of oiled cling film and leave it in a warm place until it's doubled in size.

4 Preheat the oven to 200°C/400°F/Gas 6. Cook the loaf in the centre of the oven for 20 minutes, then reduce the temperature to 180°C/350°F/Gas 4 and cook for a further 20–30 minutes or until the loaf has risen and feels hollow when it's tapped underneath. Remove the loaf from the oven and transfer it to a wire rack to cool.

## Cook's tip

• Drying saffron in the oven helps to bring out its flavour. The temperature of the oven isn't important (but not too hot), so it can be dried out while you've got the oven on for other cooking. Just take care not to leave it in for too long or it will burn.

| | |
|---|---|
| Preparation time | 15 minutes plus 1–1½ hours proving |
| Cooking time | 50 minutes |
| Calories per slice | 424 Kcal |
| Fat per slice | 15g |
| of which saturated | 7.7g |
| Serving | 8 slices |
| Suitable for freezing | |

# Lincolnshire plum bread

Tea breads feature a great deal in our national repertoire of recipes and this is one of the best, an adaptation from a recipe from The George at Stamford. It hardly needs buttering.

**Butter** 110g (4oz)
**Demerara sugar** 110g (4oz)
**Gravy browning** ½ tsp
**Eggs** 2
**Brandy** 1 tbsp
**Self-raising flour** 200g (7oz)
**Ground cinnamon** 1 tsp
**Mixed spice** ½ tsp
**Ready-to-eat prunes** 110g (4oz), chopped
**Currants** 110g (4oz)
**Sultanas** 110g (4oz)

1 Preheat the oven to 120°C/250°F/Gas ½ and butter and strip line a 900g (2lb) loaf tin along the base and up the short sides.

2 Cream the butter and sugar until light and fluffy. Add the gravy browning and beat in the eggs and brandy.

3 Sift and fold in the dry ingredients, then stir in the fruit. Spoon the mixture into the loaf tin and smooth the top. Bake for 2 hours then check and cook another 15–30 minutes. Cool in the tin and then remove and slice for serving. Butter the slices if you prefer.

## Cook's tips

• If adding gravy browning sounds strange, it's principally to darken the colour, but it does also add a subtle caramel flavour. You could leave it out or add a little black treacle and a pinch of salt.

• If you haven't got ready-to-eat prunes, soak dried prunes in warm water and stone them. The best way to do this is to snip them with scissors. The very best prunes are the Agen variety from southwest France – they melt in the mouth.

• The cake is best kept a week in an airtight tin or wrapped in foil. If you are in a hurry to eat it, you could pierce the cake in a few places, when it's cold, and pour over another tablespoon of brandy.

Preparation time – 15 minutes
Cooking time – 2½ hours
Calories per slice – 241 Kcal
Fat per slice – 9g
of which saturated – 5.2g
Makes – 1 loaf (12 slices)
Suitable for vegetarians
Suitable for freezing

# Snowballs

A familiar and popular bakery item all over Scotland, these are round iced cakes, rolled in coconut. It doesn't take much imagination to work out how (or why) they were so named!

**Plain flour** 110g (4oz)
**Self-raising flour** 110g (4oz)
**Salt** ½ tsp
**Caster sugar** 75g (3oz)
**Unsalted butter** 75g (3oz)
**Eggs** 1 plus 1 egg yolk
**Icing sugar** 150g (5oz)
**Vanilla extract** few drops
**Unsweetened desiccated coconut** 75g (3oz)

1 Preheat the oven to 200°C/400°F/Gas 6. Sift the flours and salt into a bowl and stir in the caster sugar. Rub in the butter until the mixture resembles fresh breadcrumbs and bind together with the egg and egg yolk to form a firm dough.

2 Turn onto a lightly floured surface and knead very gently until smooth. Cut into four equal pieces, and then cut each piece into four. Roll each portion into a small ball and place on a lightly greased baking sheet.

3 Bake in the oven for 12–15 minutes until golden and firm – the cakes will spread a little and flatten on the bottom during baking. Transfer to a wire rack to cool completely.

4 Sift 50g (2oz) of the icing sugar into a bowl and bind together with a little vanilla extract and sufficient water – about 1½ tsp – to form a stiff icing. Sandwich two cakes together from the flat sides with the icing to form small balls and then rest on a wire rack for about 30 minutes to set.

5 Sift the remaining icing sugar into a bowl and add a few drops of vanilla extract and about 2 tbsp water and mix to make a thinner, brushable icing. Brush the cakes all over with the icing and sprinkle with coconut. Place on a wire rack over a tray or plate to set for a further 30 minutes. Serve in cake cases if preferred.

## Cook's tips

• Allow time for the icing in the cakes to set before handling, otherwise you may find they come apart while you are coating them. Add ½ tsp finely grated lemon rind to the cake mixture for a citrusy flavour.
• Freeze the unfilled and uncoated cakes only. Allow to cool, then place in a freezer bag or in a freezer-proof container. Freeze for up to three months. Thaw at room temperature and then fill and ice as described.

| | |
|---|---|
| Preparation time | 30 minutes plus 1 hour setting |
| Cooking time | 15 minutes |
| Calories per portion | 350 Kcal |
| Fat per portion | 16g |
| of which saturated | 10.4g |
| Makes | 8 |
| Suitable for vegetarians | |
| Suitable for freezing | |

# Scottish ginger cake

Here is a scrumptiously sticky cake from the Highlands, which has the unusual addition of a tablespoon of oatmeal. The distinctive tang of ginger works really well with the texture and flavours of the dried fruit.

**Plain flour** 225g (8oz)
**Salt** ½ tsp
**Bicarbonate of soda** ½ tsp
**Ground ginger** 1 tsp
**Mixed spice** 1 tsp
**Medium oatmeal** 25g (1oz)
**Sultanas** 50g (2oz)
**Chopped mixed peel** 110g (4oz)
**Preserved stem ginger** 50g (2oz), chopped
**Treacle** 4 tbsp
**Golden syrup** 5 tbsp
**Unsalted butter** 175g (6oz)
**Soft dark brown sugar** 50g (2oz)
**Milk** 150ml (¼ pint)
**Eggs** 2

1 Preheat the oven to 150°C/300°F/Gas 2 and grease and line an 18cm (7in) square cake tin.

2 Sift the flour, salt, bicarbonate of soda, ginger and mixed spice into a bowl. Add the oatmeal, sultanas, peel and preserved ginger.

3 Gently heat the treacle, syrup, butter, sugar and milk in a saucepan, until melted. Make a well in the dry ingredients and add the eggs. Pour in the treacle mixture and mix well.

4 Pour the mixture into the cake tin and bake for 1–1¼ hours, until firm and well risen. Turn out onto a wire rack to cool.

## Cook's tips

• If you wrap in greaseproof paper and then foil and store for a couple of days, the flavour will develop further.
• To freeze, allow to cool, then cut into 12 squares. Wrap in greaseproof paper and foil and freeze for up to three months. Thaw at room temperature in the packaging.

| | |
|---|---|
| Preparation time | 15 minutes |
| Cooking time | 1¼ hours |
| Calories per slice | 242 Kcal |
| Fat per slice | 10.5g |
| of which saturated | 6g |
| Makes | 16 slices |
| | Suitable for vegetarians |
| | Suitable for freezing |

'He who first met the Highlands swelling blue Will love each peak that shows a kindred hue, Hail in each crag a friend's familiar face, And clasp the mountain in his mind's embrace. Long have I roamed through lands which are not mine. Adored the Alp and loved the Apennine.'

Lord Byron

# Somerset apple cake

This exceptionally popular cake is moist and scrumptious. Both Somerset and Dorset claim to have been responsible for its creation.

**Butter** 110g (4oz)

**Dark soft brown sugar** 175g (6oz)

**Eggs** 2, beaten

**Plain wholemeal flour** 225g (8oz)

**Mixed spice** 1 tsp

**Cinnamon** 1 tsp

**Baking powder** 2 tsp

**Cooking apples** 450g (1lb), peeled, cored and chopped

**Unsweetened apple juice** 3–4 tbsp

**Light demerara sugar** 2 tbsp

1 Preheat the oven to 170°C/325°F/Gas 3 and grease and line an 18cm (7in) round cake tin.

2 Cream the butter and sugar until pale and fluffy. Add the eggs a little at a time, beating well after each addition. Add the flour, spices and baking powder and mix well. Fold in the apples and enough apple juice to make a soft dropping consistency.

3 Turn the mixture into the prepared tin, sprinkle with demerara sugar and bake for 1¼–1½ hours, until well risen and firm to the touch. Turn out onto a wire rack to cool.

## Cook's tips

• If you want to freeze the cake, omit the demerara sugar, allow to cool, then wrap in cling film and foil. Freeze for up to three months. Thaw at room temperature, in the packaging, then decorate with the sugar.

• This cake is best consumed within two days of being made.

| | |
|---|---|
| Preparation time | 20 minutes |
| Cooking time | 1¼–1½ hours |
| Calories per slice | 292 Kcal |
| Fat per slice | 11g |
| of which saturated | 6.2g |
| Serving | 10 slices |
| Suitable for vegetarians | |
| Suitable for freezing | |

# Westmorland pepper cake

The North West region of England produces a huge variety of fruit cakes. This version from southern Cumbria is unusual, with the addition of pepper, but especially tasty.

**Butter** 75g (3oz)
**Raisins** 75g (3oz)
**Currants** 75g (3oz)
**Caster sugar** 110g (4oz)
**Self-raising flour** 225g (8oz)
**Ground ginger** $\frac{1}{2}$ tsp
**Ground cloves** $\frac{1}{2}$ tsp
**Finely ground black pepper** $\frac{1}{2}$ tsp
**Milk** 4 tbsp
**Egg** 1, beaten

1 Preheat the oven to 180°C/350°F/Gas 4 and grease and line a deep 18cm (7in) round cake tin.

2 Put the butter, fruit, sugar and 150ml ($\frac{1}{4}$ pint) water in a saucepan and bring to the boil. Simmer for 10 minutes and then leave to cool for 10 minutes.

3 In a large bowl, mix the flour, spices and pepper. Gently stir in the fruit mixture, milk and egg. Mix thoroughly, without beating.

4 Pour the mixture into the prepared tin and bake in the oven for about 45 minutes, until firm and golden brown. Turn out and leave to cool on a wire rack.

## Cook's tip

• Serve a slice of this delicious cake with a chunk of Lancashire cheese

| | |
|---|---|
| Preparation time | 20 minutes |
| Cooking time | 45 minutes |
| Calories per slice | 285 Kcal |
| Fat per slice | 9g |
| of which saturated | 5.3g |
| Makes | 1 cake (12 slices) |
| Suitable for vegetarians | |
| Suitable for freezing | |

# Dundee cake

Named after the Scottish town of Dundee, this is a rich fruited cake with a golden brown colour. The top of the batter has concentric circles of almonds placed on before baking, which makes this cake instantly recognisable.

**Currants** 110g (4oz)

**Raisins** 110g (4oz)

**Sultanas** 110g (4oz)

**Chopped candied peel** 110g (4oz)

**Blanched almonds** 25g (1oz), chopped

**Plain flour** 275g (10oz)

**Butter** 225g (8oz)

**Light soft brown sugar** 225g (8oz)

**Orange** 1, finely grated rind only

**Lemon** 1, finely grated rind only

**Eggs** 4

**Blanched almonds** about 32, to decorate

## Cook's tip

• Check the cake after 2 hours, and then every 10 minutes afterwards until it is cooked.

| | |
|---|---|
| Preparation time | 30 minutes |
| Cooking time | 2½ hours |
| Calories per slice | 341 Kcal |
| Fat per slice | 16g |
| of which saturated | 8.1g |
| Makes | 1 cake (16 slices) |
| Suitable for vegetarians | |
| Suitable for freezing | |

1 Preheat the oven to 170°C/325°F/Gas 3 and grease and line a deep 20cm (8in) round cake tin.

2 Mix the fruit, peel and chopped almonds with the flour.

3 Cream together the butter, sugar, orange and lemon rinds until pale and fluffy. Then gradually beat the eggs into the mixture. Fold in the fruit and flour mixture.

4 Spoon the mixture into the tin and make a slight hollow in the centre. Arrange the whole almonds on the top.

5 Bake in the oven for 2–2½ hours, until firm to the touch. If the top gets too brown, cover with paper. Leave to cool in the tin for 30 minutes and then turn out onto a wire rack to cool completely.

# Wet Nellie

This is the local 'affectionate' name for a Liverpudlian speciality – Lord Nelson cake: a pastry case enclosing a mixture of cake crumbs, dried fruit and golden syrup – a bit like golden syrup tart. It is moist and quite sweet, so don't stint on the lemon juice.

**Ready-made shortcrust pastry** 500g (1lb 2oz)
**Madeira cake** 250g (9oz)
**Lemon** 1 large, grated rind and juice
**Raisins or currants** 110g (4oz)
**Golden syrup** 110g (4oz), warmed
**Milk** 5 tbsp
**Caster sugar** 1 tsp

1 Preheat the oven to 190°C/375°F/Gas 5 and put a baking sheet in the oven to heat up.

2 Take off a third of the pastry and set aside. Roll out the larger piece fairly thinly to a round to line six 10cm (4in) loose-bottomed fluted flan tins. Trim off excess pastry round the top and keep the trimmings.

3 Crumble the cake into a bowl. Add the lemon rind and juice, raisins or currants, syrup and 4 tbsp of the milk. Mix well and spoon into the pastry cases, smoothing the top.

4 Add the trimmings to reserved pastry and roll out thinly to cut rounds just big enough to make the lids. Trim off excess pastry and press the edges gently to seal. Brush the tops with the rest of the milk. Sprinkle with caster sugar.

5 Place the tarts on the hot baking sheet and bake for 20–25 minutes until they are golden brown. Leave to cool in the tins for at least 10 minutes. Remove and serve warm or they are just as delicious eaten cold.

## Cook's tips

• If you don't have any Madeira cake, buy half a one at a supermarket or use a pack of mini fairy cakes or trifle sponges.
• Warm the syrup (lid loosened) in the tin in the oven as then it is easier to measure out (oil the weighing scale pan to prevent sticking) and easier to mix in with the rest of the ingredients.

| | |
|---|---|
| Preparation time | 30 minutes |
| Cooking time | 25 minutes |
| Calories per tart | 455 Kcal |
| Fat per tart | 19g |
| of which saturated | 8.1g |
| Makes | 6 tarts |
| | Suitable for vegetarians |
| | Suitable for freezing |

91

# Delicious dinners

This section has classic combinations such as mint with lamb, or steak and mushroom, along with unusual, equally enticing pairings, such as hazelnuts in veggie burgers, capers with Suffolk skate, lemon with char fish, brandy with pheasant, apple with bacon, and apricots with lamb.

# Filo-wrapped goats' cheese

Herds of dairy goats are widespread in Wales, and many cheeses are made from their milk. Using a flavoured goats' cheese gives instant flavour, but you can use a plain cheese and add some freshly chopped herbs.

**Filo pastry** 1 sheet
**Butter** 15g (½oz), melted
**Welsh goats' cheese** with garlic and chives 125g packet
**Plum chutney** 2 tbsp
**Freshly ground black pepper**

1 Preheat the oven to 200°C/400°F/Gas 6 and butter a baking sheet.

2 Working on one parcel at a time so that the pastry doesn't dry out, cut one sheet of pastry in half and brush one half very sparingly with melted butter. Cut the cheese in half and place one piece centrally on the pastry. Spoon half the chutney on top and season with a little pepper. Gather up the pastry to cover the filling, rather like a purse. If there is a lot of pastry at the top, trim the pastry if necessary.

3 Place the parcel on the baking sheet. Repeat to make a second parcel. Dab the parcels with a little extra butter. Cook in the centre of the oven for 12–15 minutes, or until the pastry is a light golden colour. Remove from the oven and serve immediately accompanied with salad.

'Up, up! ye dames, ye lasses gay!
To the meadows trip away.
'Tis you must tend the flocks this morn,
And scare the small birds from the corn.
Not a soul at home may stay:
For the shepherds must go
With lance and bow
To hunt the wolf in the woods to-day.'

Samuel Taylor Coleridge

## Cook's tip

• The parcels may be made a few hours in advance and kept chilled in the fridge so that they just need cooking before serving.

| | |
|---|---|
| Preparation time | 10 minutes |
| Cooking time | 15 minutes |
| Calories per parcel | 289 Kcal |
| Fat per parcel | 20g |
| of which saturated | 12.9g |
| Makes | 2 parcels |

# Rumbledethumps

Originating from the Border regions of Scotland, this is one of the many national dishes containing the Scots' much loved potato.

**Mashing potatoes**, such as Maris Piper 450g (1lb)
**Salt and freshly ground black pepper**
**Green or white cabbage** 450g (1lb)
**Milk** 2 tbsp
**Unsalted butter** 25g (21oz)
**Chopped chives** 4 tbsp
**Scottish Cheddar cheese** 75g (3oz), grated

## Cook's tips

• If preferred, omit the cheese and serve the mashed vegetables as a simple side dish.
• Alternatively, for a non-vegetarian version, add freshly cooked crispy bacon to the mash and cabbage mixture .

| | |
|---|---|
| Preparation time | 15 minutes plus 10 minutes standing |
| Cooking time | 30 minutes |
| Calories per portion | 225 Kcal |
| Fat per portion | 12g |
| of which saturated | 7.4g |
| Serves | 4 |
| Suitable for vegetarians | |

1 Peel the potatoes and cut into small pieces. Place in a saucepan with ½ tsp salt and cover with water. Bring to the boil and cook for 10–12 minutes until tender. Drain well and leave in the colander for 10 minutes to dry.

2 Meanwhile, trim any damaged outer leaves from the cabbage. Remove the core, and then slice the leaves finely. Bring a large pan of lightly salted water to the boil and add the cabbage; cover and cook for 5 minutes until just tender. Drain well, shaking to remove excess water.

3 Preheat the grill to a medium/hot setting. Return the drained potatoes to the saucepan and mash well with the milk and butter. Season well. Mix the cabbage and chives into the mashed potato and place in an ovenproof shallow dish. Sprinkle with grated cheese.

4 Cook under the grill for about 5 minutes until melted, golden and bubbling. Serve in individual ovenproof dishes with grilled tomatoes on the vine, or as a side dish to accompany stews.

# Hazelnut veggie burgers

Hazelnuts, also called filberts, are grown in Kent. The nuts have a creamy, earthy flavour, and are popular in chocolate recipes. Here they give a real nuttiness to these burgers.

**Olive oil** 5 tbsp
**Onion** 1, peeled and finely chopped
**Celery** 1 stick, trimmed and finely chopped
**Carrot** 1, peeled and grated
**Whole blanched hazelnuts** 100g packet
**Mixed pulses** 420g can
**Chopped parsley** 3 tbsp
**Salt and freshly ground black pepper**
**Wholemeal flour** 2 tbsp

1 Heat 1 tbsp oil in a frying pan and gently fry the vegetables, stirring, for 5 minutes until softened but not browned. Set aside to cool.

2 Meanwhile, finely grind half the hazelnuts in a blender or spice grinder, and chop the remainder. Heat a frying pan for about 2 minutes until very hot and then add the ground and chopped nuts. Cook, stirring constantly, for about 2 minutes, until the nuts turn light brown. Transfer to a heatproof plate and allow to cool.

3 Drain and rinse the pulses, and mash well using a potato masher or large fork, or purée in a blender or food processor for a few seconds to make a thick paste.

4 When the vegetables and nuts are cool, place in a bowl and add the mashed pulses, parsley and plenty of seasoning. Mix well, using the pulses to hold the mixture together. Cover and chill for 1 hour.

5 Divide the mixture into four equal portions and form each into a 10cm (4in) burger – if the mixture sticks to your hands, it will help if you wet them with cold water. Put the flour on a plate and season. Lightly coat each burger on both sides with the flour.

6 Heat the remaining oil in a large frying pan and gently fry the burgers for 10–12 minutes, carefully turning using a fish slice, until lightly golden on both sides. Drain well. The burgers are ideal served in a fresh roll with crispy salad, or as a main meal with accompanying vegetables.

## Cook's tips

• These burgers are quite rich so are best served with a fruit sauce or jelly such as cranberry or redcurrant.
• 'Toasting' the hazelnuts in a dry frying pan helps develop their flavour.

| | |
|---|---|
| Preparation time | 20 minutes plus cooling and 1 hour chilling time |
| Cooking time | 20 minutes |
| Calories per portion | 396 Kcal |
| Fat per portion | 31g |
| of which saturated | 3.1g |
| Serves | 4 |
| Suitable for vegetarians | |

# Wensleydale tart

Wensleydale cheese is thought to have been developed during the Norman Conquest. Norman soldiers stationed in the North complained bitterly about the local food so King William persuaded local monks, based in Wensleydale, to make cheese for the troops.

**Ready–rolled shortcrust pastry** ½ pack
**Butter** 50g (2oz)
**Onions** 225g (8oz), peeled and finely chopped
**Grated nutmeg** ½ tsp
**Plain flour** 3 tbsp
**Milk** 300ml (½ pint)
**Salt and freshly ground black pepper**
**Wensleydale cheese** 75g (3oz), grated
**Breadcrumbs** 15g (½oz)

1 Preheat the oven to 200°C/400°F/Gas 6. Line and grease a 25cm (10in) flan tin with the pastry and bake blind for 15 minutes by lining the pastry case with greaseproof paper and filling with baking beans or rice.

2 Meanwhile, melt 25g (1oz) of the butter in a saucepan and cook the onions gently for about 5 minutes, until soft. Remove the onions from the pan and reserve on a plate while making the sauce. Preheat the grill to a moderate heat.

3 Add the remaining butter to the saucepan with the nutmeg, cook gently for about 30 seconds and then stir the flour into the butter. Gradually add the milk, stirring continuously, until it forms a smooth paste. Season and return the onions to the pan with half of the cheese. Cook for 1–2 minutes.

4 Spoon the hot sauce into the pastry case and sprinkle on the breadcrumbs and remaining cheese. Place on a grill pan and grill for around 5 minutes, until golden brown. Serve hot with roasted root vegetables or cold with a salad.

## Cook's tips

• For a stronger flavour, replace the Wensleydale with mature Cheddar cheese.
• If you enjoy the flavour of mustard, spread the base of the pastry tart with your favourite before adding the sauce.

| | |
|---|---|
| Preparation time | 5 minutes |
| Cooking time | 30 minutes |
| Calories per portion | 312 Kcal |
| Fat per portion | 20g |
| of which saturated | 11.3g |
| Serves | 6 |
| Suitable for vegetarians | |

# Leek and pea flan

This unusual flan, using the famous Welsh leek, is really easy to make and has the added bonus of being perfect for a vegetarian meal. Serve the flan with a crisp oven-baked potato and large colourful salad.

**Leeks** 4, trimmed, washed and sliced
**Fresh or frozen peas** 110g (4oz)
**Milk** 150ml (¼ pint)
**Double cream** 150ml (¼ pint)
**Eggs** 3
**Salt and freshly ground black pepper**
**Plain wholemeal flour** 175g (6oz)
**Caerphilly cheese** 150g (5oz), grated
**Butter** 75g (3oz), cut into cubes

## Cook's tip

• For a stronger flavour, choose a mature Cheddar in place of the Caerphilly.

| | |
|---|---|
| Preparation time | 30 minutes |
| Cooking time | 50 minutes |
| Calories per portion | 467 Kcal |
| Fat per portion | 35g |
| of which saturated | 19g |
| Serves | 6 |
| Suitable for vegetarians | |
| Suitable for freezing | |

1 Preheat the oven to 190°C/375°F/Gas 5. Boil some water in a large saucepan and add the leeks and peas. Simmer for around 5 minutes, until tender. Drain well.

2 In a blender or food processor, purée the leeks, peas, milk and cream. Beat two of the eggs into the purée and season to taste.

3 Pour the leek mixture into a large bowl. Rinse and dry the food processor and add the flour and 110g (4oz) of the cheese. Mix together and then add the cubes of butter, pulsing the food processor until the mixture resembles fine breadcrumbs. Add the remaining egg and mix until a dough forms.

4 Roll out the pastry on a lightly floured surface and use to line a 23cm (9in) flan tin. Pour the leek mixture into the flan case.

5 Sprinkle with the remaining cheese and bake for 40–50 minutes, until set and golden.

DELICIOUS DINNERS

# Suffolk skate with caper sauce

Go for a walk along the beach in Aldeburgh and you can often buy freshly caught skate straight from the fishermen's huts – there's nothing fresher! Taking only 20 minutes from start to finish, you can enjoy a delicious supper in no time at all.

**Plain flour** 2 tbsp
**Salt and freshly ground black pepper**
**Skate wings** 2 small or 1 large, halved
**Butter** 110g (4oz)
**White wine vinegar** 2 tbsp
**Capers** 2 tbsp, rinsed well and drained
**Parsley** to garnish
**Lemon wedges** to serve

1 Tip the flour onto a plate and season it with salt and pepper. Pat the skate dry and dust both sides with the seasoned flour.

2 Heat half the butter in a large frying pan and cook the skate for 4–5 minutes on each side. Remove the wings from the pan and keep them warm while making the butter sauce.

3 Add the remaining butter to the pan and heat until it foams and starts to turn to a golden brown colour, then pour in the vinegar and add the capers and parsley, Season the sauce to taste. Place the cooked skate on plates and spoon the sauce over the top. Garnish with a sprig of parsley and serve with a lemon wedge and new or mashed potatoes and peas.

## Cook's tip

• If your frying pan isn't large enough to cook both skate wings at the same time, then cook them individually rather than having them overlapping in the pan.

| | |
|---|---|
| Preparation time | 5 minutes |
| Cooking time | 15 minutes |
| Calories per portion | 593 Kcal |
| Fat per portion | 46g |
| of which saturated | 28.8g |
| Serves | 2 |

# Smoked finnan haddock

Finnan haddock originates from the small fishing town of Findon, south of Aberdeen. It was originally smoked over peat fires, and although once a rarity, it is now widely produced. In Scotland, finnan haddock has long been a favourite breakfast dish.

**Finnan haddocks** 2, each about 250g (9oz), heads removed
**Bay leaf** 1
**Freshly ground black pepper**
**Milk** 300ml (½ pint)
**Butter** 25g (1oz)
**Plain flour** 25g (1oz)
**Eggs** 2, hardboiled, shelled and finely chopped
**Chopped parsley** 1 tbsp

1 Place the haddock, skin side down, in a large frying pan. Add the bay leaf and some black pepper and then add the milk. Bring to the boil, cover and then simmer gently for 10 minutes, until tender.

2 Transfer the fish to a warmed serving plate and reserve the milk. Cover and keep warm.

3 Melt the butter in a saucepan. Add the flour and cook gently, stirring continuously for 1 minute. Remove from the heat and gradually stir in the reserved milk. Bring the sauce to the boil, stirring all the time, and then simmer for 2–3 minutes. Add the eggs and parsley to the sauce and stir. Serve the hot sauce with the fish. Accompany with wilted spinach and boiled potatoes.

## Cook's tip

• If you are unable to obtain finann haddock, buy any un-dyed smoked haddock.

| | |
|---|---|
| Preparation time | 10 minutes |
| Cooking time | 15 minutes |
| Calories per portion | 409 Kcal |
| Fat per portion | 20g |
| of which saturated | 10g |
| Serves | 2 |

# Trout with a soufflé topping

Originally the trout for this recipe would have been caught from the Lakes. Do try to buy organic trout rather than the farmed fish. Serve with steamed sugarsnap peas.

**Trout** 4 trout fillets

**Butter** 25g (1oz)

**Plain flour** 2 tsp for cooking, 1 tbsp for coating

**Semi-skimmed milk** 150ml (¼ pint)

**Eggs** 2, separated but only 1 yolk retained

**Double Gloucester cheese** 40g (1½oz), grated

**Grated nutmeg** good pinch

**Salt and freshly ground black pepper**

1 Check the fish over thoroughly for bones and remove any with tweezers. Wash and dry the trout. Preheat the oven to 200°C/400°F/Gas 6.

2 To make the sauce, melt 15g (½oz) of the butter in a pan, stir in the 2 tsp of flour and cook for a minute not letting it brown. Add the milk gradually, beating it in to make a smooth sauce. Remove from the heat. Cool for a minute and then beat in the egg yolk and then the cheese, nutmeg and seasoning.

3 Put 1 tbsp of flour on a plate and mix in seasoning. Coat the opened-out trout in the flour and shake off the surplus. Heat the remaining butter in a frying pan and when it sizzles add the trout and cook them for about a minute on each side. Lay the fish side by side in a buttered baking dish or in two individual dishes.

4 Whisk the egg whites until stiff. Fold a little into the sauce to slacken it, then fold in the rest of the whites. Spoon the mixture over the trout to cover them completely. Bake for 10–12 minutes until the soufflé is puffed up and golden brown. Serve immediately.

## Cook's tips

• This recipe is also good with lemon or Dover sole

• Get the fishmonger to bone the fish for you, or, if doing it yourself, slit the fish completely along the belly, turn it backbone up on a board and press along the backbone to loosen it and carefully pull it out and check for stray bones.

• Use up the extra egg yolk in hollandaise sauce, add to mashed potato or use with whole eggs for scrambling or in pastry.

• This recipe was traditionally made using single cream – lovely, but not as light as using milk.

| | |
|---|---|
| Preparation time | 15 minutes |
| Cooking time | 20 minutes |
| Calories per portion | 548 Kcal |
| Fat per portion | 30g |
| of which saturated | 14.5g |
| Serves | 2 |

# Trout wrapped in bacon

A simple dish enjoyed by Welsh farmers, using freshly caught river trout and home-cured bacon. Use ready-prepared trout and good quality smoked bacon for a simple supper.

**DELICIOUS DINNERS**

**Trout** 4, each weighing about 275g (10oz), cleaned, heads, tails, fins removed and boned

**Salt and freshly ground black pepper**

**Thin smoked streaky bacon** 8 rashers, stretched with the back of a knife

**Watercress** to garnish

1 Preheat the oven to 200°C/400°F/Gas 6. Season the cavity of each fish with salt and pepper and place in a shallow ovenproof dish, lined with foil.

2 Place two rashers of bacon across each fish. Bake in the oven for about 20 minutes, until the fish is cooked. Garnish with sprigs of watercress and serve with new potatoes, green beans and broccoli.

## Cook's tips

• You can grill the fish, if you prefer the bacon to be crisper.

• For a variation, fill the cavity of each fish with a few slices of peeled apple and a sprig of mint.

| | |
|---|---|
| Preparation time | 10 minutes |
| Cooking time | 20 minutes |
| Calories per portion | 306 Kcal |
| Fat per portion | 14g |
| of which saturated | 4.5g |
| Serves | 4 |

**DELICIOUS DINNERS**

# Scottish salmon fish pie

Swede or turnip and potatoes are known as neeps and tatties in Scotland and are the traditional accompaniment to haggis. Mashed together they make a delicious topping for another traditional ingredient – Scottish salmon.

**Swede** ¼, peeled and cut into chunks

**Potatoes** 3, peeled and cut into chunks

**Milk** 600ml (1 pint)

**Scottish salmon fillet** 400g (14oz)

**Eggs** 4, hard-boiled, peeled and quartered

**Cornflour** 2 tbsp

**Water** 3 tbsp

**Chopped parsley** 2 tbsp

**Salt and freshly ground black pepper**

**Butter** 50g (2oz), melted

**Scottish Cheddar cheese** 50g (2oz), grated

**1** Place the swede in a saucepan, cover with water and bring to the boil and then leave to simmer for 5 minutes. Add the potatoes to the pan, cover again and simmer for a further 20 minutes or until the vegetables are tender.

**2** Meanwhile, pour the milk into a saucepan and add the salmon. Bring to the boil, then reduce the heat and simmer the fish gently for 4–5 minutes or until the salmon is cooked. Remove the pan from the heat and use a slotted spoon to lift the fish out of the milk.

**3** Remove any skin from the fish and flake the fish into large chunks into a 2 litre (3½ pint) ovenproof dish. Add the quartered eggs to the dish.

**4** Mix the cornflour with 3 tbsp water. Bring the milk to the boil and slowly pour in the cornflour, stirring well to give a smooth sauce. Simmer the sauce for about 1 minute until it's thickened, then stir in the parsley and season it to taste. Pour the sauce over the fish in the dish.

**5** Preheat the oven to 200°C/400°F/Gas 6. Drain the vegetables well and add the melted butter and seasoning. Mash the vegetables until smooth, then spoon them over the top of the fish mixture. Sprinkle the grated cheese over the top.

**6** Bake the pie in the centre of the oven for 20–25 minutes until the topping is golden in colour and the filling is starting to bubble. Remove from the oven and serve with green salad.

## Cook's tip

• Any fish may be substituted for the salmon, so it's an ideal recipe for using any fish that's on special offer.

| | |
|---|---|
| Preparation time | 25 minutes |
| Cooking time | 50 minutes |
| Calories per portion | 608 Kcal |
| Fat per portion | 35g |
| of which saturated | 14.8g |
| Serves | 4 |

# Lakeland char with sauce

Char, a fish rather like trout, is a delicacy served in many restaurants in the Lake District – where it is mostly found in Lake Windermere. When available, it can be bought in specialist fishmongers and select supermarkets.

**DELICIOUS DINNERS**

**Butter** 110g (4oz)

**Onion** 1 large, peeled and very finely chopped

**White breadcrumbs** 75g (3oz)

**Finely chopped parsley** 4 tbsp, plus extra for garnish

**Lemons** 2, finely grated rind and juice of 1, the other cut into wedges

**Egg** 1 large, beaten

**Coarse sea salt and freshly ground black pepper**

**Char or trout** 4 (about 200g/7oz each), gutted, washed and dried, heads, tails and fins removed

**Wholegrain mustard** 1 tsp

**Chopped capers** 1 tbsp

1 Preheat the oven to 220°F/425°C/Gas 7. Melt 25g (1oz) of the butter in a small frying pan, add the onion and cook gently until softened, but not browned. Remove the pan from the heat, add the breadcrumbs, 3 tbsp of the parsley, grated lemon rind and beaten egg. Mix well, season to taste, then allow to cool.

2 Pat the fish dry with kitchen paper, season the insides well, and fill with the stuffing mixture. Smooth the belly flaps over the stuffing, then place the fish in a buttered ovenproof baking dish. Season, cover with foil and bake for 10 minutes. Remove the foil and bake for a further 5–10 minutes or until the skin is crispy and the flesh looks opaque and flakes easily.

3 Meanwhile, place the remaining butter in a small saucepan, add the lemon juice and mustard and stir with a whisk over a moderate heat until melted and smoothly blended – do not overheat as the sauce may separate. Season and then stir in the capers and remaining parsley. Cover and keep warm until the fish are cooked. Garnish the fish with parsley, and serve accompanied with the butter sauce.

## Cook's tip

• If char isn't readily available, you can also make this recipe using trout.

| | |
|---|---|
| Preparation time | 30 minutes |
| Cooking time | 20 minutes |
| Calories per portion | 487 Kcal |
| Fat per portion | 31g |
| of which saturated | 16.2g |
| Serves | 4 |

# Oyster and seafood feast

The town of Colchester was granted its rights to its oyster fisheries by Richard I in 1189. On 12 August, these rights are confirmed by the town clerk before the oyster season is opened. This is followed by a toast in gin to the Queen and by the first dredging of oysters.

**Live mussels** 1kg (2lb 3oz)

**White wine or water** 150ml (¼ pint)

**Onion** 1 small, peeled and roughly chopped

**Parlsey and thyme** 1 large sprig of each

**Live oysters** 6–12, opened, top shells reserved

**Coarse sea salt** for oysters, if grilling

**Mayonnaise** 150ml (5fl oz)

**Tomato purée** 2 tbsp

**Worcestershire sauce** 1 tsp

**Lemon** 1, 1–2 tsp of juice and wedges

**Light olive oil** 6 tbsp

**White wine vinegar** 2–3 tbsp

**Finely chopped parsley** 3 tbsp plus sprigs for garnish

**Finely chopped dill** 1 tbsp plus sprigs for garnish

**Fresh, crusty brown bread** bought or homemade (see recipe on page 56)

Optional extra seafood feast

**Cooked crab** 1 medium-large, ready dressed

**Egg** 1 large, hard-boiled and shelled

**Shell-on, cooked prawns** 250g (9oz), washed and dried

**Peeled, cooked prawns** 225g (8oz)

**Cockles** 225g (8oz)

**Cooked lobster** 1 large, prepared

## Cook's tips

• If you do not have an oyster knife, a fishmonger will open them for you.
• Although freshly cooked shellfish is best, thawed, frozen shellfish may be used instead.

| | |
|---|---|
| Preparation time | 1½ hours |
| Cooking time | 10 minutes |
| Calories per portion | 326 Kcal |
| Fat per portion | 31g |
| of which saturated | 4.8g |
| Serves | 6 |

1 To prepare the mussels see Mussel and onion stew on page 108. Put the mussels into a large saucepan. Pour the wine or water over the mussels, then add the onion and herbs. Cover the pan with a tightly fitting lid and bring up to the boil, shaking the pan frequently. Reduce the heat and cook for a further 2–3 minutes until all the mussels are opened.

2 Pour the cooked mussels into a large colander, placed over a bowl, and leave to drain and cool while preparing the remaining ingredients.

3 To cook oysters, preheat the grill to high. Sprinkle a liberal layer of sea salt in the bottom of a flame/heatproof, shallow baking dish. Remove the flat 'lids' from the oysters and set aside. Place the oysters in their shells on the bed of salt, then cook for 2 minutes under the hot grill, or until their edges start to curl up – take care not to overcook or they will become tough. Replace the 'lids', leave to cool and then refrigerate until serving.

4 To make the mayonnaise sauce, place the mayonnaise, tomato purée, Worcestershire sauce and lemon juice together in a bowl and whisk together well. Season to taste with a little freshly ground black pepper if wished.

5 To make the vinaigrette dressing, put the oil, vinegar and herbs into a small bowl, season well and whisk well. Transfer the sauces to serving bowls, cover and chill while assembling all the shellfish.

6 Arrange all the shellfish attractively on a large platter, together with the optional extras. Garnish with lemon wedges, parsley and dill and serve accompanied with the sauces and crusty bread. Cooked oysters may be served in their baking dish.

# Mussel and onion stew

The South West contains almost 30% of designated shellfish waters in England and Wales. Mussels are readily available and surprisingly easy to cook, so why not try them? This stew is rich and thick and perfect for a mid-winter supper.

**Fresh mussels** 2kg (4½lb)

**Dry white wine** 150ml (¼ pint)

**Butter** 25g (1oz)

**Onions** 2 large, peeled and chopped

**Plain wholemeal flour** 25g (1oz)

**Milk** 300ml (½ pint)

**Chopped parsley** 2 tbsp plus sprigs for garnish

**Single cream** 2 tbsp

1 To prepare the mussels, wash them thoroughly under cold running water, then scrape off any barnacles with a sharp knife and pull away the fibrous beards that protrude from between the shells. Wash in several changes of water. Discard any that are cracked or do not close when tapped sharply with a knife.

2 Place the mussels in a very large saucepan and add the wine. Cover the pan with a tight-fitting lid, place over a moderately high heat and cook for 4–5 minutes, shaking the pan frequently, until all the mussels have opened.

3 Place a large colander over a large bowl and line with muslin or kitchen paper. Pour the mussels into the colander and leave to drain and cool a little.

4 Keep a few mussels in shells back for garnish, remove the rest from their shells, discarding any that have not opened.

5 Melt the butter in a large saucepan, add the onions and cook gently until soft but not browned. Add the flour, stirring continuously, and then the milk and 1 pint of the mussel cooking liquid (add more milk if you do not have a pint). Bring to the boil, stirring, until the sauce thickens.

6 Add the mussels and parsley to the sauce and heat gently for just 2 minutes. Stir in the cream, garnish with parsley sprigs and serve immediately with crusty bread.

## Cook's tip

• After the mussels have been cooked, some of them may not have opened up very far. Don't force them open, but discard as they, too, might not be fresh enough to eat.

| | |
|---|---|
| Preparation time | 45 minutes |
| Cooking time | 30 minutes |
| Calories per portion | 214 Kcal |
| Fat per portion | 9g |
| of which saturated | 5.1g |
| Serves | 4 |

# Herby Norfolk turkey steaks

Norfolk is a region renowned for turkey rearing and two well-known breeds of turkey are the Norfolk Black and the Norfolk Bronze. These turkey steaks are served with a crunchy crumb and deep red tomato sauce.

**Butter** 75g (3oz)

**Onion** 1, peeled and chopped

**Caster sugar** 1 tbsp

**Plum tomatoes** 500g (1lb 2oz), skinned and chopped

**Tomato purée** 2 tbsp

**Chopped basil** 4 tbsp plus leaves to garnish

**Salt and freshly ground black pepper**

**Plain flour** 2 tbsp

**Egg** 1, lightly beaten

**White breadcrumbs** 75g (3oz)

**Chopped parsley** 2 tbsp

**Turkey steaks** 4

**Sunflower oil** 1 tbsp

**Spaghetti** 225g (8oz)

## Cook's tip

• The tomato sauce will keep well in the fridge for up to 4 days, so it may be made in advance. The whole recipe is not suitable for freezing, but the sauce may be packed and sealed in a freezer container for up to one month.

| | |
|---|---|
| Preparation time | 20 minutes |
| Cooking time | 40 minutes |
| Calories per portion | 483 Kcal |
| Fat per portion | 22g |
| of which saturated | 11g |
| Serves | 4 |

1 To make the sauce, melt 25g (1oz) of the butter in a saucepan and add the onion and sugar and cook for 8–10 minutes until the onion has softened and just started to caramelise.

2 Add the tomatoes and tomato purée to the pan and cook the sauce gently for 15–20 minutes until the tomatoes have softened and the sauce has thickened slightly. Stir in half the chopped basil and seasoning to taste just before serving.

3 For the turkey, tip the flour onto a plate and season it with salt and pepper. Place the egg in a shallow wide bowl. Mix together the breadcrumbs, parsley and basil on a plate and add seasoning. Coat the turkey steaks first in a light dusting of the seasoned flour, then dip it in the egg and then in the breadcrumb mixture.

4 Melt the butter in a frying pan and add the oil. When hot, add the turkey to the pan and cook for 4–5 minutes on each side, until the turkey is cooked through. To test if the turkey is ready, pierce it with the point of a fine knife and if the juices run clear, it's ready, but if they have any colour, cook the turkey for longer.

5 Cook the spaghetti as instructed on the packet, toss with some of the sauce then spoon the rest over the turkey steaks and garnish with basil leaves.

DELICIOUS DINNERS

# Raised chicken and ham pie

The practice of cooking meat inside a pastry crust dates back to Roman times. However, the art of making hand-raised pies with fillings, such as pork and veal, is a legacy from the Middle Ages, when the pastry cases were known as 'coffyns'.

**Boneless, skinless chicken meat** 800g (1lb 12oz), cut into 2.5cm (1in) cubes

**Smoked gammon** 2 thick slices (around 250g/9oz), rinds removed and cut into 1.5cm (½in) cubes

**White wine** 3 tbsp

**Olive oil** 1 tbsp

**Mixed dried herbs** 1 tsp

**Chopped parsley** 3 tbsp

**Green or pink peppercorns in brine** 2–3 tsp

**Plain flour** 275g (10oz)

**Salt and freshly ground black pepper**

**Milk** 150ml (¼ pint)

**White vegetable fat** 110g (4oz), plus extra for greasing mould

**Egg** 1 small, beaten for glazing

**Gelatine** 2 tsp

**Chicken stock** 150ml (¼ pint)

**24 x 10 x 7cm (9½ x 4 x 2¾in) greased raised pie mould or loaf tin**

## Cook's tips

• Making a raised pork pie cannot be done in a hurry! It is best done at a more leisurely pace, taking two to three days with its various stages – during which time its flavour is greatly improved.

• To ensure easy removal of the pie from the mould, line the tin with non-stick baking foil.

• The pie will keep for up to three days in the fridge.

| | | |
|---|---|---|
| Preparation time | – | 4½ hours (in stages) plus 2 days chilling, and maturing |
| Cooking time | – | 1½ hours |
| Calories per portion | – | 582 Kcal |
| Fat per portion | – | 28g |
| of which saturated | – | 7g |
| Serves | – | 6 |

1 Place the chicken and gammon in a large bowl and add the wine, oil, herbs and peppercorns. Mix well, cover and refrigerate for at least 2 hours, or overnight.

2 To make the pastry, sift the flour and 1 tsp salt into a bowl and make a well in the centre. Heat the milk and vegetable fat in a saucepan until the fat melts, then bring to the boil. Pour into the flour and mix. Cover the dough and leave to stand until cool.

3 Preheat the oven to 200°C/400°F/Gas 6. Turn the dough onto a floured surface and knead until smooth. Cut off a quarter, wrap in cling film and set aside. Roll the larger piece of dough into an oblong large enough to cover the base and sides of the loaf tin, with a little overhanging. Carefully line the tin. Season the meat, then carefully place in the lined tin and spread out evenly.

4 Roll out the remaining pastry large enough to cover the pie. Brush the edges of the pastry in the tin with cold water, then cover with the pastry top, pressing the edges well together, to seal. Trim off the excess pasty. Brush with egg.

5 Decorate the top edges of the pie by pinching the pastry between your thumb and forefinger. Make a 5mm/¼in hole in the centre of the pastry lid and then make two more, evenly spaced. Insert a piece of foil into each hole. Place the pie on a baking tray and cook in the oven for 30 minutes. Reduce the heat to 180°C/350°F/Gas 4 and cook for another hour.

6 Remove the pie from the oven and leave it to stand for 10–15 minutes. Remove the tin's sides and brush all over with beaten egg. Continue cooking for 20 minutes or until a skewer, when inserted into the centre, feels very hot when placed on the back of your hand. Allow the pie to cool, cover and chill overnight.

7 The next day, pour 3 tbsp of cold water in a small bowl, sprinkle gelatine over the surface and leave to stand until it is swollen and looks opaque. Stand the bowl in a pan of simmering water until the gelatine is melted and hot. Stir into the stock.

8 Remove the pie from the refrigerator and remove the foil from the holes. Then, with a small funnel, pour the stock into the pie – stopping when the jelly is level with the top of each hole. cover and chill for another 24 hours before serving.

# Stoved chicken

Sometimes referred to as 'stovies', this recipe was originally named because it would have been cooked on top of the 'stove'. This modern version is extremely simple to make and yet it is truly scrumptious.

**Butter** 25g (1oz)

**Vegetable oil** 1 tbsp

**Chicken legs** 4

**Lean back bacon** 4 rashers

**Large floury potatoes** 4 (about 1.1kg/2½lb), peeled and cut into 5mm (¼in) slices

**Onions** 2, peeled and sliced

**Salt and freshly ground black pepper**

**Thyme** 5 sprigs

**Chicken stock** 600ml (1 pint) or 900ml (1½ pints) if making in individual pots

## Cook's tips

• You may need to add more chicken stock if it dries out too much. Check halfway through cooking.

• If you prefer the potatoes to be browned on top, put the casserole under the grill for a few minutes before serving.

| | |
|---|---|
| Preparation time | 20 minutes |
| Cooking time | 2½ hours |
| Calories per portion | 630 Kcal |
| Fat per portion | 31g |
| of which saturated | 10.2g |
| Serves | 4 |
| Suitable for freezing | |

1 Preheat the oven to 150°C/300°F/Gas 2. In a large frying pan, heat half of the butter and all the oil and fry the chicken and bacon for 5 minutes, until lightly browned.

2 Place half of the potatoes in a layer at the bottom of a large casserole dish or individual containers. Then cover with half the onion slices. Season well, add the thyme sprigs and drizzle with some of the buttery juices from the frying pan.

3 Add the chicken and bacon and drizzle with the remaining pan juices. Cover with the rest of the onions and finally the rest of the potatoes. Season and dot with butter. Add the chicken stock.

4 Cover and bake in the oven for around 2 hours, until the chicken and potatoes are tender. Serve with carrots and swede.

# Chicken and Cumberland sauce

This tangy sauce was served cold on the menu of the Café Royal in London to accompany baked ham and is said to have been named after Queen Victoria's uncle, the Duke of Cumberland. If time permits, make the sauce the day before in order to give good flavour.

**Redcurrant jelly** 225g (8oz)
**Ruby port** 6 tbsp
**Worcestershire sauce** 1 tsp
**Lemon** ½ tsp finely grated rind, 1 tbsp juice, rest cut into wedges for serving
**Orange** ½ tsp finely grated rind, 1 tbsp juice, rest cut into wedges for serving
**Mushroom ketchup** 1 tsp, optional
**Chicken breasts (with bone and skin)** 4
**Plain flour** 1 tbsp
**Cayenne pepper** ½ tsp
**Salt and freshly ground black pepper**
**Unsalted butter** 25g (1oz), melted
**Chopped parsley** to garnish

1 To make the sauce, melt the redcurrant jelly with the port in a saucepan over a gentle heat and then raise the temperature. Boil for 5 minutes until thickened and syrupy. Remove from the heat and transfer to a heatproof bowl or jug. Leave to cool for 10 minutes.

2 Stir in the Worcestershire sauce, ½ tsp lemon and orange rind and juice and ketchup, if using. Mix well. Leave to cool completely, stirring occasionally to distribute the rind. Cover and chill until required.

3 For the chicken, preheat the oven to 190°C/375°F/Gas 5. Wash and pat dry the chicken breasts and place in a shallow roasting tin. In a small bowl, mix together the flour, cayenne and seasoning. Brush the chicken with melted butter and sprinkle with the seasoned flour.

4 Bake in the oven for about 40 minutes until golden, tender and cooked through. Drain and serve hot with the cold Cumberland sauce and steamed baby carrots tossed in butter, lemon wedges and sprinkled with lemon rind.

## Cook's tip

• The sauce will keep well for up to two weeks if sealed in a clean jar and kept in the fridge.

| | |
|---|---|
| Preparation time | 15 minutes plus cooling and chilling time |
| Cooking time | 45 minutes |
| Calories per portion | 399 Kcal |
| Fat per portion | 9g |
| of which saturated | 4.5g |
| Serves | 4 |

113

# Boozy roast pheasant

DELICIOUS DINNERS

A favourite with the landed gentry, roast pheasant would have been served after a day out riding across the moors. Here they are wrapped with bacon to keep the breasts moist and then finished with a rich sauce flamed with brandy and a dash of Madeira and cream.

**Fresh pheasants** 1 brace, rinsed with cold water then dried with kitchen towel
**Butter** 50g (2oz)
**Salt and freshly ground black pepper**
**Thyme** small bunch
**Smoked streaky bacon** 8 rashers
**Watercress** to garnish
**Cup mushrooms** 110g (4oz), sliced
**Plain flour** 2 tbsp
**Brandy** 2 tbsp
**Chicken stock** 300ml (½pint)
**Madeira or Marsala wine** 3 tbsp
**Double cream** 3 tbsp

## Cook's tip

• It is important that the brandy is bubbling before you set fire to it. If the alcohol content isn't heated sufficiently, it won't set alight.

| | |
|---|---|
| Preparation time | 20 minutes |
| Cooking time | 1 hour |
| Calories per portion | 539 Kcal |
| Fat per portion | 33g |
| of which saturated | 15.8g |
| Serves | 4 |

1 Preheat the oven to 190°C/375°F/Gas 5. Put the pheasants in a roasting tin, spread the butter over the breasts and legs and then season lightly and top each bird with a few sprigs of thyme. Lay the bacon rashers on top and loosely cover with foil.

2 Roast for 45 minutes. Remove the foil, lift the bacon off the pheasant breasts and leave in the tin. Spoon the meat juices over and roast for 15 minutes more until browned and the meat juices run clear when the larger pheasant is tested with a skewer through the leg into the breast.

3 Garnish with watercress then transfer to a serving plate. Add the mushrooms to the meat juices in the roasting tin and fry for 3 minutes until golden.

4 Stir in the flour then add the brandy. When bubbling, flame with a match and stand well back. After the flames have subsided, stir in the stock and wine, bring to the boil, stirring until smooth. Mix in the cream and season to taste.

5 Pour the sauce into a sauceboat. Carve the pheasant or cut into joints with poultry shears. Spoon around the sauce to serve.

# Honeyed duck breasts

Gressingham ducks are derived from the wild Mallard. They are exclusively reared in Suffolk and they've been bred to produce more meat and have a lower fat content than other duck varieties. They have a thin skin, which is deliciously crispy when cooked.

**Gressingham duck breasts** 2
**Salt** ½ tsp
**Honey** 2 tbsp
**English ready-made mustard** 1 tbsp
**Orange** 1, zest and juice
**Red wine vinegar** 2 tbsp
**Caster sugar** 2 tbsp
**Chicken stock** 150ml (¼ pint)

1 Use a sharp knife to score the fat on the duck breasts and rub the salt into the skin. Heat a large saucepan and add the duck breasts, fat side down, and cook over a high heat for 4–5 minutes to crisp the skin, and so the excess fat will run out of the breasts.

2 Turn over the breasts and cook for 1–2 minutes on the other side to lightly brown the meat. Remove the duck breasts from the pan and transfer them to a small roasting tin, skin side up.

3 Preheat the oven to 200°C/400°F/Gas 6. Mix together 1 tbsp of the honey with the mustard and orange zest and spread the mixture over the duck breasts. Place the tin in the oven and cook the duck for 15–20 minutes, or until cooked to your liking.

4 Meanwhile, drain most of the fat from the frying pan and add the vinegar and caster sugar, stir to mix well and then cook over a gentle heat, without stirring, until the sugar has caramelised. Remove the pan from the heat and add the orange juice, taking care if it splatters and stir until it's mixed.

5 Add the remaining honey and chicken stock and simmer gently until the sauce thickens. Serve the duck breast on a bed of steamed fine asparagus with the sauce poured or spooned over the top. Roasted baby new potatoes are a good accompaniment.

## Cook's tip

• If you like a sticky sauce, then just boil it longer so that it thickens into a glossy coating sauce rather than a runny gravy.

| | |
|---|---|
| Preparation time | 5 minutes |
| Cooking time | 30 minutes |
| Calories per portion | 502 Kcal |
| Fat per portion | 31g |
| of which saturated | 8.2g |
| Serves | 2 |

# Pot roast pork with red cabbage

This recipe from the eastern counties is perfect for a warming supper in winter. It is quick to prepare, just pop it in the oven and curl up with a good book.

**Red cabbage** ½ cabbage, shredded
**Cooking apple** 1, peeled, cored and sliced
**Red onion** 1, peeled and sliced
**Raspberry or red wine vinegar** 3 tbsp
**Demerara sugar** 2 tbsp
**Sultanas** 75g (3oz)
**Salt and freshly ground black pepper**
**Boneless pork shoulder** 1.5kg (3lb), trimmed

1 Preheat the oven to 180°C/350°F/Gas 4. Place the cabbage, apple, onion, vinegar, sugar and sultanas in a deep lidded casserole. Season and mix well.

2 Wash the pork and pat dry. Season all over. Place on top of the cabbage and push down. Cover with the lid and bake for about 2 hours, until tender.

3 Serve the pork sliced on a warm serving platter, surrounded by cabbage. Accompany with mashed potatoes.

## Cook's tip

• For variety, use prunes instead of sultanas with the cabbage.

Preparation time – 20 minutes
Cooking time – 2 hours
Calories per portion – 388 Kcal
Fat per portion – 11g
of which saturated – 3.5g
Serves – 6

# Pork and honey casserole

If you can, use Somerset honey for this casserole. Its strong taste perfectly complements the rich flavour of the pork and tart apple juice in this wholesome dish.

**Olive oil** 1 tbsp

**Pork loin or thick loin steaks** 750g (1lb 10oz), cut into cubes

**Dried haricot beans** 225g (8oz), soaked overnight in cold water

**Clear honey** 1 tbsp

**Chicken stock** 600ml (1 pint)

**Apple juice** 300ml (½ pint)

**Bouquet garni**

**Onion** 1, peeled

**Cloves** 4

**Carrots** 3, peeled, cut into 5cm (2in) lengths and then into quarter wedges

**Leeks** 2, trimmed, washed and sliced

**Celery sticks** 2, sliced

**Worcestershire sauce** 2 tbsp

**Tomato purée** 1 tbsp

**Salt and freshly ground black pepper**

1 Heat the oil in a large flameproof casserole or saucepan. Add the pork and cook, until lightly browned.

2 Drain the beans and add to the pork with the honey, stock, apple juice and bouquet garni. Stud the onion with the cloves and add to the casserole. Bring to the boil, cover closely with greaseproof paper and the lid and simmer for 1 hour, until the beans are just tender.

3 Add the carrots, leeks and celery with the Worcestershire sauce and tomato purée. Season to taste. Continue simmering for a further 15–30 minutes or until the beans are really tender. Remove the cloves from the onion and cut it into four. Return to the casserole. Discard the bouquet garni and cloves and serve hot with warm bread.

## Cook's tips

• To make a bouquet garni simply tie together four sprigs of fresh parsley or chervil, one sprig of fresh thyme and a bay leaf. It may help to hold them together if you sandwich the herbs between two sticks of celery and then tie with string. If you attach the other end of the string to the saucepan handle, it is easy to fish out afterwards!
• You can buy Somerset honey in most supermarkets – just look at the labels on the jars.

| | |
|---|---|
| Preparation time | 30 minutes |
| Cooking time | 1 hour 45 minutes |
| Calories per portion | 711 Kcal |
| Fat per portion | 35g |
| of which saturated | 12.2g |
| Serves | 4 |

# Ham and pease pudding

Pease pudding has been served for generations in County Durham. It is a versatile dish which can be served hot or cold, as told in the nursery rhyme 'Pease pudding hot, pease pudding cold/Pease pudding in the pot, nine days old.' It probably originated from the tradition of selling cooked peas with bacon from a stall during the reign of James I.

**Yellow split peas** 450g (1lb), soaked overnight

**Onion** 1 large, peeled and roughly chopped

**Unsmoked rindless streaky bacon** 4 rashers, roughly chopped

**Salt and freshly ground black pepper**

**Unsmoked gammon joint** 750g (1lb 10oz)

**Bay leaves** 2

**Cloves** 4

**Cornflour** 2 tbsp

**Milk** 300ml (½ pint)

**Chopped parsley** 2 tbsp plus sprigs for garnishing

**Worcestershire sauce** 1 tsp

**Butter** 15g (½oz)

1 Drain the peas and place in a large saucepan. Add the onion and bacon to the saucepan with 2 tsp salt, and pour in sufficient water to come at least 2.5cm (1in) above the peas. Bring to the boil, and cook in rapidly boiling water for 10 minutes.

2 Reduce to a gentle simmer and continue to cook for about 50 minutes, stirring occasionally, until the peas are a purée and most of the liquid has been absorbed. Drain if necessary.

3 Meanwhile, wash and pat dry the gammon. Bring a large saucepan of water to the boil, and add the gammon, bay leaves, cloves and 1 tsp salt. Cover and simmer gently for about 1 hour 10 minutes until tender and cooked through.

4 Remove from the heat and stand, covered, for 15 minutes. Drain the gammon, reserving the cooking liquid. Cover and keep warm. Discard the bay leaves and cloves.

5 In another saucepan, blend the cornflour with a little of the milk to form a smooth paste. Stir in the remaining milk and 300ml (½ pint) of the reserved stock. Heat, stirring, until the mixture boils, and then simmer for 1 minute until thickened. Remove from the heat, season and stir in the chopped parsley. Keep warm.

6 To serve, add Worcestershire sauce and butter to the pea mixture and adjust the seasoning if necessary. Slice the gammon into thick slices. Pile pease pudding on to warm serving plates and top each with a few slices of gammon. Serve with the parsley sauce drizzled over and a sprig of fresh parsley.

## Cook's tip

• Traditionally, the peas were put into a pudding cloth and cooked in the water along with the meat, but you do need quite a large saucepan to do this successfully. If preferred, you could cook the gammon joint first and use the cooking water to cook the peas in and to add more flavour to the finished dish.

| | |
|---|---|
| Preparation time | 20 minutes plus overnight soaking and 15 minutes standing time |
| Cooking time | 1 hour 15 minutes |
| Calories per portion | 797 Kcal |
| Fat per portion | 26g |
| of which saturated | 11.3g |
| Serves | 4 |

# Painswick bacon chops

Painswick is perhaps the quintessential example of a Gloucestershire Cotswold village, with old stone cottages, narrow winding streets and a church. The churchyard is famous for its yew trees, of which some people say there are 99 as the devil uproots any more that are planted. This Painswick recipe is easy to prepare and perfect for a mid-week meal.

DELICIOUS DINNERS

**Bacon chops** 4, each about 110-150g (4-5oz)
**English mustard** 1 tbsp
**Demerara sugar** 25g (1oz)
**Dry cider** 300ml (½ pint)
**Butter** 15g (½oz)
**Plain flour** 1½ tbsp
**Salt and freshly ground black pepper**

1 Preheat the oven to 200°C/400°F/Gas 6. Place the chops in a large ovenproof dish, side by side.

2 Mix the mustard and sugar with 2 tbsp of the cider to make a smooth paste. Spread the paste over the chops and leave to marinate for 30 minutes.

3 Bake the chops in the oven for 15 minutes. Meanwhile, pour the remaining cider into a saucepan and add the butter and flour. Heat, whisking continuously, until the sauce thickens, boils and is smooth. Simmer for 1–2 minutes and then season to taste.

4 Pour the sauce over the chops and bake for a further 15 minutes until they are cooked. Serve with chunky chips, peas and grilled halved tomatoes.

## Cook's tip

• You can use pork chops instead of the bacon chops in this recipe or halved gammon steaks.

| | |
|---|---|
| Preparation time | 10 minutes plus 30 minutes marinating |
| Cooking time | 35 minutes |
| Calories per portion | 352 Kcal |
| Fat per portion | 22g |
| of which saturated | 9g |
| Serves | 4 |

# Toad in the hole

This British batter pudding used to be made with all sorts of meat as it was a good way of making a little go a long way. Today, it is most familiar made with lamb chops or sausages, baked in a large dish. This version makes individual sausage and onion puddings.

**Plain flour** 110g (4oz)
**Salt and freshly ground black pepper**
**Dried thyme** 1 tsp
**Egg** 1
**Milk** 300ml (½ pint)
**Onion** 1
**Good quality thick beef sausages** 8
**Olive oil** 1 tbsp

1 Sift the flour with ½ tsp salt into a bowl. Make a well in the centre, add the thyme, egg and a quarter of the milk. Gently mix the flour into the liquid. Gradually whisk in the remaining milk to form a smooth batter. Transfer to a jug and let stand for 30 minutes.

2 Meanwhile, preheat the oven to 200°C/400°F/Gas 6. Peel and slice the onion. Arrange in the large Yorkshire pudding tins (each tin usually has four indents) and put the sausages on top. Drizzle with olive oil and bake for 10 minutes.

3 Turn the sausages over, stir the batter and pour over. Stand on a baking sheet and bake in the oven for a further 15–20 minutes until risen, crisp and golden.

4 To serve, place the puddings on warm serving plates and pile high with accompanying vegetables. Serve with a rich beef and onion gravy and a good dollop of horseradish sauce. Note: the batter will sink down on standing.

## Cook's tips

• To make a quick beef and onion gravy, peel and chop 1 onion. Melt 25g (1oz) butter in a saucepan and cook the onion for 3–4 minutes until just softened. Stir in 2 tbsp plain flour and cook, stirring, for 1 minute. Remove from the heat and gradually stir in 450ml (16fl oz) beef stock or half beef stock and half red wine. Return to the heat and bring to the boil, stirring, and cook for 1 minute to thicken slightly. Serve with the sausage puddings.

• This dish can also be cooked in a small roasting tin measuring 22 x 17cm (9 x 7½in), cooking the sausages with the batter for 40–45 minutes. The initial sausage cooking time remains the same.

| | |
|---|---|
| Preparation time | 10 minutes plus 30 minutes standing |
| Cooking time | 25 minutes |
| Calories per portion | 276 Kcal |
| Fat per portion | 18g |
| of which saturated | 6.7g |
| Makes | 8 portions |
| Suitable for freezing | |

# Huntingdon fidget pie

Onions and apples both grow well in Cambridgeshire and work wonderfully with the bacon in this regional favourite. These pies would originally have been baked for the hungry workers at harvest time.

**Plain flour** 250g (9oz) plus 25g (1oz) for sauce

**Salt and freshly ground black pepper**

**Butter** 125g (4½oz), diced

**Rindless bacon** 250g (9oz), roughly chopped

**Onion** 1, peeled and roughly chopped

**Cooking apples** 2, peeled, cored and roughly chopped

**Chopped parsley** 4 tsp

**Medium dry cider** 150ml (¼ pint)

**Chicken stock** 150ml (¼ pint)

**Egg** 1, beaten

1 Preheat the oven to 190°C/375°F/Gas 5. To make the pastry, sift 250g (9oz) of the flour and a pinch of salt into a large bowl. Add the butter and rub in until it resembles fine breadcrumbs. Stir in 2–3 tbsp cold water to mix to a firm dough. Knead the dough lightly then wrap in foil and chill until needed.

2 Meanwhile, combine the bacon, onion and apple in a bowl and divide between four individual 400ml (14fl oz) pie dishes. Add the parsley and season to taste.

3 Put the remaining flour into a bowl and add the cider, a little at a time, mixing well. Pour the cider mixture into the pie dishes.

4 Roll out the pastry onto a lightly floured surface. Cut out strips long enough to go around the rims of the pie dishes. Moisten the rims with water and place the strips on the rims. Press down lightly all the way round. Cut circles of pastry to form the pie lids. Moisten the pastry strips, place the lids on top, trim off excess pastry and press to seal. Cut a cross in the centre of each pie and fold the pastry back to reveal a square of filling.

5 Brush the pastry with beaten egg and then bake in the oven for around 30 minutes, until the pastry is golden and the filling is cooked, covering with foil after 20 minutes if they appear to be browning too quickly. The pies can be served hot with vegetables or cold with salad.

## Cook's tips

• If you do not want to use cider, you can use vegetable stock.

• A variation on the filling is to replace the two apples with one cooking apple and one large baking potato.

| | |
|---|---|
| Preparation time | 15 minutes |
| Cooking time | 30 minutes |
| Calories per pie | 525 Kcal |
| Fat per pie | 28g |
| of which saturated | 14.3g |
| Makes | 4 pies |

121

# Leek and bacon roly poly

Suet puddings were once the glories of British cooking. Despite a good suet crust being light and pleasant to eat, suet puds are often avoided as they are seen as unhealthy. This is a modernised version using lower fat vegetable suet. The pudding is steamed in the oven as it's easier and you don't have to keep topping up the pan with boiling water.

**Gammon steaks** 2, chopped

**Leeks** 1–2 (about 250g/9oz), washed well and finely sliced

**Salt and freshly ground black pepper**

**Self-raising flour** 250g (9oz)

**Reduced fat vegetable suet** 125g (4½oz)

**Chopped parsley** 3 tbsp

1 Preheat the oven to 190°C/375°F/Gas 5. Get a large roasting tin and rack and two large sheets of foil, one of them buttered.

2 To make the filling, add the gammon pieces to a pan and dry fry for 3–4 minutes. Add the leeks and cook for about 5 minutes, stirring occasionally until the leeks wilt. Season and set aside.

3 To make the suet pastry, mix together the flour and suet in a bowl, add the parsley and seasoning. Stir in just over 150ml (¼ pint) cold water, with a round-bladed knife, to make a soft dough. Knead very lightly on a floured surface and roll out to a 23cm (9in) square.

4 Dip your finger in water and dampen all around the pastry edge. Spread the bacon and leek mixture over, leaving the border uncovered. Roll up the pastry like a Swiss roll and seal the ends. Place this on the buttered sheet of foil. Bring the foil up around the roll in a baggy parcel so there is room for the pastry to rise a little. Seal the ends and top well.

5 Put the parcel on the rack in the roasting tin. Pour boiling water round to half fill the tin then quickly cover the whole tin with the other sheet of foil, sealing it well to retain the steam. Carefully carry the tin to the oven and bake for 2 hours.

6 Take out and leave for 5 minutes before unwrapping – watch out, it will still be hot. Place on a serving platter, slice and serve with more vegetables.

## Cook's tips

• This is another recipe that you can make with whatever you have to hand. Leftover gammon would be fine.

• For a vegetarian option, use onion rather than leeks, or with the leeks, and substituting some cheese and/or sweetcorn for the meat.

| | |
|---|---|
| Preparation time | 30 minutes |
| Cooking time | 2 hours 10 minutes |
| Calories per portion | 468 Kcal |
| Fat per portion | 26g |
| of which saturated | 7.5g |
| Serves | 4 |

# Minty lamb patties

Wales is famous for its mountains, valleys, rivers, and of course its lamb. For centuries it has been home to several breeds of sheep. They have thrived on the natural grassland available all year round, in one of the most unspoilt environments in the world. Welsh lamb is considered to have a good colour and a sweet, succulent flavour.

**Minced lamb** 450g (1lb)

**Onion** 1 small, peeled and finely chopped

**Breadcrumbs** 110g (4oz)

**Lemon** ½, finely grated rind only

**Chopped mint** 3 tbsp

**Egg** 1, beaten

**Plain flour** 2 tbsp

**Cucumber** ½, cut into 5cm (2in) lengths and then into quarter wedges

**Spring onions** 6, trimmed and cut into 5mm (¼in) pieces

**Chicken stock** 200ml (7fl oz)

**Dry sherry** 1 tbsp

1 In a large bowl, mix the lamb, onion, breadcrumbs, lemon rind, 1 tbsp of the mint and the egg. Shape the mixture into eight flatish balls and coat in the flour.

2 Dry fry the patties in a large, lidded frying pan for about 5 minutes, until browned all over. Add the cucumber, spring onions, stock and sherry and the remaining mint. Bring to the boil. Cover and simmer for 20 minutes, until the meat is tender. Serve with peas.

## Cook's tip

• If you are cooking for two, follow the recipe above but only fry four of the patties. Wrap the remaining four (unfloured) in cling film and freeze until required. Defrost overnight in the fridge and grill for 10–15 minutes, until browned. Serve in burger buns with a large salad.

| | |
|---|---|
| Preparation time | 10 minutes |
| Cooking time | 30 minutes |
| Calories per portion | 386 Kcal |
| Fat per portion | 17g |
| of which saturated | 7.9g |
| Serves | 4 |
| Suitable for freezing | |

# Oxford John steaks

Oxford John is the local name for a lamb leg steak in the markets of Oxford. These lamb steaks are served with a tasty caper sauce. This recipe is simple to prepare, so it's ideal for a quick and easy supper.

**Lamb leg steaks** 4, each weighing about 175g (6oz)
**Salt and freshly ground black pepper**
**Butter** 25g (1oz)
**Plain flour** 1 tbsp
**Lamb or beef stock** 300ml (½ pint)
**Drained capers** 2 tbsp
**Vinegar from capers** 1 tbsp

1 Season the lamb steaks. Heat the butter in a frying pan and fry the steaks gently for 10–15 minutes, turning occasionally, until browned on both sides. Remove with a slotted spoon and keep warm.

2 Add the flour to the pan and cook for 1–2 minutes, stirring. Gradually add the stock, stirring continuously, until the sauce boils and thickens. Add the capers and vinegar and simmer for 1–2 minutes.

3 Return the lamb steaks to the pan and simmer for 5 minutes or until the lamb is cooked to your liking. Serve hot with new potatoes and sautéed leeks.

## Cook's tip

• If you would like to make your sauce a little more colourful and have some added flavour, replace some of the stock with red wine.

| | |
|---|---|
| Preparation time | 15 minutes |
| Cooking time | 30 minutes |
| Calories per portion | 390 Kcal |
| Fat per portion | 27g |
| of which saturated | 13.9g |
| Serves | 4 |

# Lamb with cherries

Kent is blessed with a mild climate and rich soil, in which many fruits thrive. The county was awash with cherry orchards until recent times, when labour-intensive harvesting became too expensive. Here, the cherries are combined with lamb in a fruity casserole.

**Rindless streaky bacon** 175g (6oz), diced

**Butter** 15g (½oz)

**Boneless leg or shoulder of lamb** 680g (1½lb), cut into cubes

**Onion** 1, peeled and chopped

**Carrot** 1, peeled and sliced

**Celery stick** 1, sliced

**Garlic** 1 clove, finely chopped

**Red wine** 450ml (16fl oz)

**Redcurrant jelly** 2 tbsp

**Bouquet garni**

**Grated nutmeg** ¼ tsp

**Salt and freshly ground black pepper**

**Red cherries** 300g (11oz), stoned

**Rosemary sprigs** to garnish

## Cook's tip

• To freeze, cool and then transfer to a rigid freezer container. Cover and freeze for up to three months. Defrost overnight in the fridge and re-heat gently in a covered saucepan for about 20 minutes, stirring occasionally. Ensure the lamb is piping hot before serving.

| | |
|---|---|
| Preparation time | 20 minutes |
| Cooking time | 2¾ hours |
| Calories per portion | 545 Kcal |
| Fat per portion | 35g |
| of which saturated | 16.2g |
| Serves | 4 |

1 Preheat the oven to 150°C/300°F/Gas 2. In a frying pan, fry the bacon for 2–3 minutes. Add the butter and lamb and cook, stirring, for 5 minutes, until brown all over. Remove the lamb and bacon with a slotted spoon and put in a lidded casserole dish.

2 In the remaining fat, fry the onion, carrot, celery and garlic for about 5 minutes, until soft. Add the vegetables to the casserole dish.

3 Pour the wine into the casserole and add the redcurrant jelly, bouquet garni, nutmeg and seasoning. Cover and bake for around 2 hours. Stir the cherries into the casserole and continue to cook for around 30 minutes until the meat is tender and the cherries have softened. Discard the bouquet garni and serve hot with steamed green beans and garnished with rosemary sprigs.

125

# Roast lamb with apricots

Inspired by the Herdwick sheep grazing on the Lakeland hills, this recipe using saddle of lamb was devised for a country house hotel in Cumbria as their signature dish. This is a modern, simplified version of that dish.

**Leg of lamb** 1.8kg (4lb), or shoulder, boned out

**Salt and freshly ground black pepper**

**Spinach leaves** 110g (4oz)

**Ready-to-eat dried apricots** 175g (6oz), chopped

**Onion** 1, peeled and finely chopped

**Breadcrumbs** 75g (3oz)

**Chopped mint** 2 tbsp fresh or 1–2 tsp dried

**Egg** 1, beaten

**Olive oil**

**Lamb or vegetable stock** 300ml (½ pint)

**Port** 150ml (¼ pint)

**Cornflour or gravy granules**

**Mint sprigs** to garnish

1 Preheat the oven to 200°C/400°F/Gas 6. Flatten the lamb as best you can, check for tough tendons or bones and remove them. Season well. Wash the spinach leaves and then put them in a large pan over a fairly high heat and let them wilt down for a minute. Cut out thick stalks. Arrange half the leaves to cover the inside of the lamb.

2 To make the stuffing, in a bowl mix the chopped apricots, onion, breadcrumbs, mint and just enough egg to make a light stuffing. Spread the mixture over the spinach layer on the lamb then cover with the rest of the spinach leaves. Roll it up, securing with string.

3 Put the stuffed lamb in a roasting tin, sprinkle with a little oil and seasoning. Cover with foil and cook for 90 minutes. Remove the foil and cook another 15 minutes to brown the meat. Leave to stand, wrapped in the foil, for 10 minutes before carving.

4 Bring the lamb stock and port to the boil in a saucepan and reduce it by a third. Add any meat juices from the roasting tin without adding too much fat. Thicken with cornflour or gravy granules. Serve with roast potatoes and parsnips together with some green vegetables and mint sprigs to garnish.

## Cook's tips

• Don't worry if you can't get the lamb to roll all round the filling, it looks good with filling 'oozing' out of the top.

• This is a good dish for a Sunday lunch when you have lots of family or guests to feed as it is easy to carve, looks colourful and the stuffing ekes out the meat a bit further. It is also very tasty served cold.

| | |
|---|---|
| Preparation time | 20 minutes |
| Cooking time | 1¾ hours plus standing |
| Calories per portion | 499 Kcal |
| Fat per portion | 24g |
| of which saturated | 11.3g |
| Serves | 8 |

'That valleys, groves, hills and fields,
Woods, or steepy mountain yields.
And we will sit upon the rocks,
Seeing the shepherds feed their flocks
By shadow rivers, to whose falls
Melodious birds sing madrigals.'
Christopher Marlowe

# Lamb stew and dumplings

Stew and dumplings are a national institution and most regions have their own version. This one originally used mutton (but we've used lamb) with stout. The dumplings contain breadcrumbs with lemon rind, which makes them lovely and light.

**Plain flour** 2 tbsp

**Salt and freshly ground black pepper**

**Leg of lamb** 650–700g (about 1½lb), diced

**Beef dripping** 25g (1oz)

**Onion** 1 large, peeled and sliced

**Lamb or beef stock** 600ml (1 pint)

**Stout** 150ml (¼ pint)

**Potato** 1 large (about 400g/14oz), peeled and diced

**Carrot** 1 large, peeled and diced

**Self-raising flour** 50g (2oz)

**Breadcrumbs** 50g (2oz)

**Finely grated lemon rind** 2 tsp

**Egg** 1

**Milk** 2 tbsp

**Button mushrooms** 110g (4oz), wiped and halved

**Frozen peas** 110g (4oz)

## Cook's tips

• If you want to try the stew with mutton, cook it for 2 hours before adding the mushrooms, peas and dumplings.

• There is a lot of gravy with this stew but you need a fair amount of liquid to create enough steam to cook the dumplings so choose a casserole dish with a lid that fits well.

• Don't be tempted to add more than 150ml (¼ pint) stout to any casserole. Too much brings a bitterness to the dish. Just enjoy drinking the rest of the bottle.

Preparation time – 30 minutes
Cooking time – 2 hours
Calories per portion – 518 Kcal
Fat per portion – 23g
of which saturated – 10.8g
Serves – 5
Suitable for freezing

1 Put the flour into a bowl and season. Then toss the meat in the flour. Heat half the dripping in a large frying pan and add the meat in one layer (or cook it in two batches). Cook until it browns underneath then turn it over for another couple of minutes. Remove from the pan to a casserole.

2 Add the rest of the dripping and the onion and fry for 5 minutes. Pour in the stock, stout and more seasoning. Bring to the boil then add the diced potato and carrot. Cover and turn down the heat as low as you can and cook for 1½ hours.

3 To make the dumplings, mix together the flour, breadcrumbs and lemon rind. Add the egg and enough milk to a make a soft dough. Quickly shape the dough into eight balls on a lightly floured surface.

4 Add the mushrooms and peas to the stew, bring back to the boil and then pop in the dumplings. Cover again and cook for about 30 minutes. Serve hot with freshly cooked cabbage if you like – and a glass of Guinness.

# Shepherd's pie

Shepherd's pie was traditionally a dish for Monday lunchtime, using up leftover cold roast lamb, either minced or chopped, cooked in the leftover gravy or a specially made brown béchamel sauce. Made well, it is the ultimate comfort food.

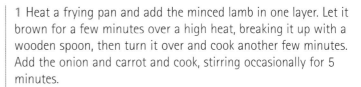

**Minced lamb** 450g (1lb)

**Onion** 1, peeled and diced

**Carrot** 1 large, peeled and diced

**Flour** 1 tbsp

**Hot lamb or vegetable stock** 300ml (½ pint)

**Bay leaf**

**Rosemary or thyme sprig** or pinch of dried thyme

**Salt and freshly ground black pepper**

**Worcestershire sauce** 1 tbsp

**Tomato ketchup (or purée)** 1 tbsp

**Potatoes** 4 (about 900g/2lb), peeled and cut into chunks

**Milk** 150ml (¼ pint)

**Butter** 50g (2oz)

**Leicester, Lancashire or Cheddar cheese** 25g (1oz), grated

1 Heat a frying pan and add the minced lamb in one layer. Let it brown for a few minutes over a high heat, breaking it up with a wooden spoon, then turn it over and cook another few minutes. Add the onion and carrot and cook, stirring occasionally for 5 minutes.

2 Sprinkle in the flour and cook for a minute then pour in the stock, add the bay leaf and rosemary or thyme, seasoning and sauces. Simmer, uncovered, for 20–25 minutes until the sauce has thickened and the carrots are softened. Remove the bay leaf and herb sprigs.

3 Meanwhile, preheat the oven to 190°C/ 375°F/Gas 5. Put a deep dish or pie dish in the oven to heat up for 5 minutes.

4 Cook the potatoes in a pan of boiling salted water for about 15 minutes until tender, drain well. Return the potatoes to the pan, over the heat, and let them dry out for half a minute then add the milk. When that comes to the boil, take the pan off the heat, add butter and plenty of seasoning and mash the potatoes well.

5 Spoon the mince mixture into the dish. Place spoonfuls of hot mash on the top and spread it over the mince carefully with a fork or palette knife to cover the meat. Sprinkle with cheese. Put the dish on a baking sheet and bake for 20–25 minutes until browned on top and piping hot. Serve with freshly cooked cabbage and broccoli.

## Cook's tips

• Some people add a can of chopped tomatoes for more colour and flavour and some crushed garlic and a pinch of cayenne, but if you have good quality mince, the Worcestershire sauce and ketchup should be fine.

• Add enough milk and butter to the mash so that it is soft enough to spread but not too soft that it sinks into the mince.

• You can speed up the cooking by grilling the pie for 5–8 minutes rather than baking it in the oven, but it does not 'meld' together quite so well.

| | |
|---|---|
| Preparation time | 30 minutes |
| Cooking time | 45 minutes |
| Calories per portion | 599 Kcal |
| Fat per portion | 30g |
| of which saturated | 16.5g |
| Serves | 4 |
| Suitable for freezing | |

# Hereford beef olives

Hereford beef is very tender, juicy and full of flavour. Wrap this delicious prime beef around a stuffing of bacon and herbs – it is this presentation that gives beef olives their name – and bake, for a wholesome evening meal.

**Rindless streaky bacon** 75g (3oz), finely chopped plus 8 rashers
**Onions** 3, 1 finely chopped, 2 sliced
**Chopped parsley** 2 tsp plus sprig for garnish
**Breadcrumbs** 110g (4oz)
**Shredded beef suet** 50g (2oz)
**Dried mixed herbs** 1/4 tsp
**Egg** 1
**Lemon** 1/2, grated rind and 1 tsp juice
**Salt and freshly ground black pepper**
**Beef** 8 slices cut from a joint of topside
**English mustard** 1 tbsp
**Plain flour** 3 tbsp
**Butter** 25g (1oz)
**Vegetable oil** 2 tbsp
**Beef stock** 750ml (1 1/4 pints)

1 Preheat the oven to 170°C/325°F/Gas 3. Mix the chopped bacon with the finely chopped onion, parsley, breadcrumbs, suet, herbs and egg. Add the lemon rind and juice and seasoning.

2 Beat each piece of meat with a meat mallet or rolling pin and spread with mustard. Divide the stuffing into eight and place on top of each piece of meat. Roll up, wrap with a rasher of bacon and secure with string.

3 Season the flour and coat each meat parcel. Heat the butter and oil in a large, shallow, flameproof casserole dish and brown the meat. Remove the meat and keep warm.

4 Stir the remaining flour into the pan and brown lightly. Slowly add the stock, stirring continuously, and bring to the boil. Return the meat to the casserole.

5 Scatter the sliced onions over the meat, cover and bake for 1 1/2 hours, until tender. Garnish with parsley and serve with mashed potato.

## Cook's tip

• If you prefer, you can buy a packet mix of stuffing, rather than all the stuffing ingredients

Preparation time – 20 minutes
Cooking time – 1 3/4 hours
Calories per portion – 670 Kcal
Fat per portion – 41g
of which saturated – 16.1g
Serves – 4
Suitable for freezing

DELICIOUS DINNERS

# Stilton steaks

Stilton was first made in the early 18th century in the Melton Mowbray area. It is named after the village of Stilton, where it was regularly sold in the market place. These steaks taste wonderful with their cheesy topping and they are very simple to make.

**Stilton cheese** 110g (4oz), crumbled
**Butter** 25g (1oz), softened
**Shelled walnuts** 75g (3oz), finely chopped
**Freshly ground black pepper**
**Fillet steaks** 4 (each weighing about 110-175g (4-6oz), trimmed
**Fried onion rings** to garnish

1 Preheat the grill. Put the cheese and butter in a bowl and mash with a fork. Add the walnuts and mix well. Season to taste.

2 Place the steaks on the grill rack. Season with pepper and cook for 5–10 minutes on each side, according to taste.

3 Sprinkle each steak with a quarter of the cheese mixture, and grill for a further minute, until the topping has melted. Serve hot with fried onion rings, new potatoes and a mixed salad.

## Cook's tip

• The Stilton topping can be prepared in advance. Shape the mixture into a roll, wrap in cling film and refrigerate until required. Slice the mixture and place on top of the steaks.

| | |
|---|---|
| Preparation time | 15 minutes |
| Cooking time | 10-20 minutes |
| Calories per portion | 443 Kcal |
| Fat per portion | 34g |
| of which saturated | 13.6g |
| Serves | 4 |

# Dorset jugged steak

When meat is 'jugged' it is usually casseroled with vegetables and cloves. This Dorset speciality was traditionally cooked on the days when the fair came to town as it cooked slowly, without spoiling, until the fair goers came home.

**Stewing steak** 680g (1½lb), cut into 2.5cm (1in) cubes
**Plain wholemeal flour** 2 tbsp
**Onion** 1, peeled and sliced
**Cloves** 4
**Salt and freshly ground black pepper**
**Port** 150ml (¼ pint)
**Beef stock** 450ml (16fl oz)
**Sausagemeat** 225g (8oz)
**Wholemeal breadcrumbs** 50g (2oz)
**Chopped parsley** 2 tbsp
**Redcurrant jelly** 1 tbsp

## Cook's tip

• For a cheaper dish, use bitter or light ale in place of the port.

| | |
|---|---|
| Preparation time | 10 minutes |
| Cooking time | 3¾ hours |
| Calories per portion | 453 Kcal |
| Fat per portion | 26g |
| of which saturated | 9.4g |
| Serves | 4 |
| Suitable for freezing | |

1 Preheat the oven to 170°C/325°F/Gas 3. Coat the meat with the flour, shaking off any excess, and put into a casserole dish. Add the onion and cloves and season.

2 Pour the port into the casserole dish and add just enough stock to cover the meat. Cover and bake in the oven for 2¾ hours.

3 Meanwhile, mix together the sausagemeat, breadcrumbs and parsley and season. With floured hands, shape the sausagemeat into eight balls.

4 Stir the redcurrant jelly into the casserole and add the sauagemeat balls. Cook, uncovered, for a further 40–45 minutes until the sausagemeat is cooked and slightly brown. Serve hot with vegetables and new potatoes.

133

# Mushroom-stuffed sirloin steaks

Sir Richard Hoghton invited King James I to join him for a 'light' lunch at Hoghton Tower, near Preston. A magnificent loin of beef was brought to the table, which so delighted the king that he knighted it there and then, saying (allegedly): 'Arise Sir Loin of Beef.'

**Butter** 15g (½oz)
**Mushrooms** 175g (6oz), wiped and finely chopped
**Garlic** 1 clove, peeled and crushed
**Onion** 1, peeled and finely chopped
**Chopped parsley** 1 tbsp
**Breadcrumbs** 1 tbsp
**Double cream** 1 tbsp
**Sirloin steaks** 4 (each about 250g/9oz)

1 Preheat the grill to moderate. Melt the butter in a saucepan and sauté the mushrooms, garlic and onion for about 5 minutes, until soft.

2 Remove the pan from the heat and add the parsley, breadcrumbs and cream. Mix well.

3 Make a horizontal cut through each steak, without slicing all the way through, and stuff a quarter of the mixture into each steak 'pocket'.

4 Grill the steaks for 5–10 minutes, turning halfway through, until the steaks are cooked to your liking. Serve with thick-cut oven chips and watercress.

## Cook's tips

• Alternatively, cook the steak on a preheated ridged pan to give an interesting finish to the meat.
• If you have any leftover bread that has gone slightly stale, don't bin it. Cut off the crusts and whiz it in your food processor. Store the crumbs in a polythene bag in the freezer. They can be used straight from the freezer for recipes such as this.

| | |
|---|---|
| Preparation time | 15 minutes |
| Cooking time | 15 minutes |
| Calories per portion | 370 Kcal |
| Fat per portion | 23g |
| of which saturated | 10.8g |
| Serves | 4 |

# Finkadella

Many of Scotland's recipes reflect its past links with France. Mary of Guise and her daughter Mary, Queen of Scots influenced cooking in the Scottish courts. The name of this dish is derived from the French *fins quenelles* – a quenelle being an oval-shaped dumpling.

**DELICIOUS DINNERS**

**Extra lean minced beef** 225g (8oz)
**White breadcrumbs** 75g (3oz)
**Single cream** 2 tbsp
**Beef stock** 600ml (1 pint)
**Shallot** 1, grated
**Shredded beef suet** 50g (2oz)
**Salt and freshly ground black pepper**
**Large carrot** 1
**Large leek** 1

1 Put the minced beef in a bowl. Mix the breadcrumbs with the cream and 6 tbsp of the stock to form a thick paste and add to the beef along with the shallot and suet. Season to taste and mix well to a form a stiff consistency.

2 Break the meat into walnut-sized pieces and form into 12 balls. Place on a plate lined with baking parchment, cover and chill for 30 minutes.

3 Meanwhile, peel the carrot and cut into very small pieces. Trim the leek and split lengthwise. Rinse under cold running water to flush out any trapped earth, and shake well to dry. Shred finely.

4 Place the vegetables in a large, deep-sided frying pan with a lid and pour over the remaining stock. Bring to a temperature just below boiling point and add the meatballs. Cover and poach gently, keeping the water below boiling point, for 15–20 minutes until cooked through. To serve, either spoon meatballs and cooking liquor into warm serving bowls and eat with crusty bread, or spoon over creamy mashed potatoes.

## Cook's tip

• For a lighter version, replace the minced beef with minced chicken and use vegetable suet.

| | |
|---|---|
| Preparation time | 20 minutes plus 30 minutes chilling |
| Cooking time | 20 minutes |
| Calories per portion | 338 Kcal |
| Fat per portion | 22g |
| of which saturated | 10.2g |
| Serves | 4 |

135

# Beef Wellington

This recipe is named after the 1st Duke of Wellington, who defeated Napoleon at Waterloo in 1815. Wellington did not create the recipe but it was said that its appearance reminded people of the leather 'Wellington' boot, worn by the duke.

**Fillet of beef** 1.4kg (3lb)
**Freshly ground black pepper**
**Vegetable oil** 1 tbsp
**Butter** 25g (1oz)
**Button mushrooms** 225g (8oz), sliced
**Smooth liver pâté** 110g (4oz)
**Ready-to-roll puff pastry** 375g pack
**Egg** 1, beaten

1 Season the beef fillet with pepper. Heat the oil and 15g (½oz) of the butter in a large frying pan. Add the meat and fry for around 5 minutes on each side. Press down with a wooden spoon while frying to seal well.

2 Wrap the fillet in cling film and place into a small loaf tin, so that the meat 'sets' into a good shape. Cool and then chill.

3 Meanwhile, add the remaining butter to the frying pan and sauté the mushrooms in the pan juices. Leave to cool and then blend with the pâté.

4 Preheat the oven to 220°C/425°F/Gas 7. On a lightly floured surface, unroll the pastry. Roll it out a little larger, if required. Spread the pâté mixture in a strip down the pastry and then place the beef on the pâté, near one short end.

5 Fold the pastry edges over the beef like wrapping a parcel, sticking edges together with egg and trimming away the bulky pieces of pastry from the ends where the pastry becomes a double thickness. Turn over the wrapped beef and put the joins underneath.

6 Brush all over with egg. Then roll out the trimmings and create pastry leaves with which to decorate the top. Brush with egg.

7 Place on a baking tray and bake for 50–60 minutes, depending on your preference, covering with foil after 25 minutes. Allow to rest for 10 minutes before serving. Serve with baby carrots with their green tops left on.

## Cook's tip

• If you do not have a great deal of time to create this dish, you can cook the meat and mushrooms the day before, cool and chill overnight in the fridge.

| | |
|---|---|
| Preparation time | 30 minutes |
| Cooking time | 1 hour 10 minutes |
| Calories per portion | 510 Kcal |
| Fat per portion | 30g |
| Of which saturated | 10.2g |
| Serves | 8 |

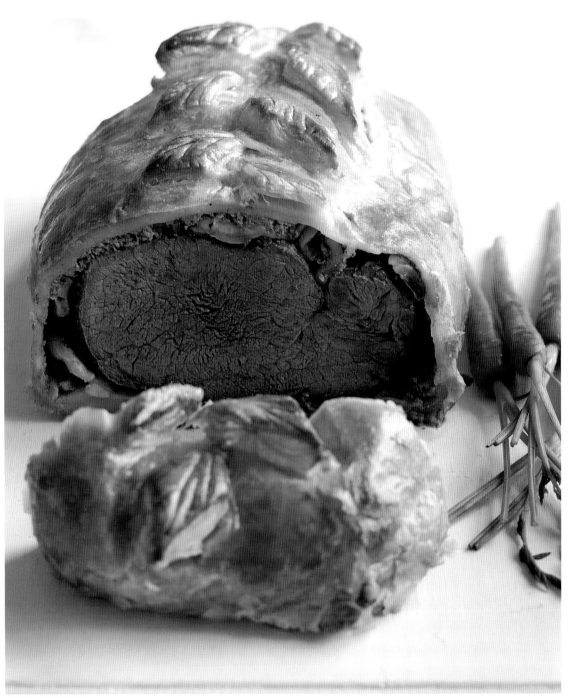

# Stuffed marrow

Welsh cheeses are slowly increasing their space in our supermarkets, as more Welsh varieties are being introduced on their cheese counters. This recipe uses a mild and creamy goats' cheese called Welsh Log (*Pant Ys Gawn*), pronounced 'pant-us-gown'!

**Peas** 110g (4oz)

**Runner beans** 150g (5oz), thinly sliced

**Olive oil** 2 tbsp

**Onion** 1 large, peeled and chopped

**Carrots** 3 large, peeled and cut into small dice

**Marrow** 1 (about 2.5kg/5lb 8oz)

**Extra lean minced beef or lamb** 500g (1lb 2oz)

**Plain flour** 25g (1oz)

**Tomatoes** 3 large, peeled, de-seeded and cut into small dice

**Tomato purée** 2 tbsp

**Beef or chicken stock** 150ml (¼ pint)

**Mixed dried herbs** 2 tbsp

**Welsh Log/Pant Ys Gawn goats' cheese** 110g (4oz), sliced

**Paprika** to garnish

1 Preheat the oven to 200°C/400°F/Gas 6. Place the peas and beans in a small saucepan, cover with cold water, bring to the boil and cook for 2 minutes. Pour into a colander, refresh under cold running water and drain well.

2 Heat the oil in a large wide frying pan, add the onion and carrots and cook gently together for 10 minutes, taking care not to let them brown. Meanwhile, cut a slice lengthways off the top of the marrow, approximately a quarter of the way down. Scoop out and discard the seeds and stringy fibres from the top and the bottom. Cut a thin sliver from the bottom of the marrow – to stop it rolling.

3 Add the beef to the frying pan and cook, stirring, until the meat changes colour. Then stir in the flour, tomatoes, tomato purée, drained peas and beans, stock and herbs.

4 Place the marrow in a large baking dish and fill with the cooked beans and peas and then add the beef mixture (if necessary, any excess filling can be cooked separately in a small, covered baking dish). Cover the filling with the top slice of marrow, and add 2–3 tbsp of water to the dish.

5 Cover the marrow closely with a sheet of foil, then cook in the centre of the oven for approximately 1½–2 hours until the marrow is cooked (time will vary according to the thickness of the marrow's flesh).

6 Remove the marrow from the oven and remove the foil. Scatter over the goats' cheese and return to the oven for 10 minutes, or until the cheese is browned. Sprinkle with paprika and serve.

## Cook's tip

• An alternative way to cook the marrow is to cut it into 5cm (2in) deep slices, hollow out the centre and fill with the beans, peas and beef mixture. Cook as in the method.

| | |
|---|---|
| Preparation time | 30 minutes |
| Cooking time | 2 hours |
| Calories per portion | 508 Kcal |
| Fat per portion | 26g |
| of which saturated | 10.3g |
| Serves | 4 |

# Teviotdale pie

Teviotdale is a valley in the Scottish borders, whose principal town is Hawick. This border country has a turbulent history, and saw numerous clashes between Scots and English. This tasty pie from the region is a great recipe for making a little meat go a long way.

DELICIOUS DINNERS

**Lean minced beef** 450g (1lb)
**Onion** 1, peeled and chopped
**Carrot** 1 large, peeled and finely chopped
**Celery** 2 sticks, finely chopped
**Beef stock** 300ml (½ pint)
**Worcestershire sauce** 1 tsp
**Salt and freshly ground black pepper**
**Self-raising flour** 225g (8oz)
**Cornflour** 25g (1oz)
**Shredded beef suet** 75g (3oz)
**Milk** 300ml (½ pint)

**1** Preheat the oven to 190°C/375°F/Gas 5. Dry fry the meat in a large saucepan for about 5 minutes, until it starts to brown. Add the onion, carrot and celery and cook for a further 5 minutes, until softened.

**2** Pour the stock into the pan and add the Worcestershire sauce. Season to taste and simmer for 15 minutes, until just tender.

**3** Meanwhile, put the flour, cornflour and suet in a bowl and gradually add the milk, stirring well, to form a thick batter. Season well.

**4** Put the meat and vegetables in a 1.1 litre (2 pint) pie dish and cover with the batter mixture. Stand on a baking tray and cook in the oven for about 35 minutes, until risen, crusty and browned.

## Cook's tip

• To freeze, allow to cool completely in the dish. Wrap in foil and freeze for up to three months. Defrost in its packaging, in the fridge overnight. Re-heat, covered in foil, for 25–30 minutes at 180°C/350°F/Gas 4, removing the foil for the last 5 minutes.

Preparation time – 15 minutes
Cooking time – 1 hour
Calories per portion – 623 Kcal
Fat per portion – 29g
of which saturated – 13.1g
Serves – 4
Suitable for freezing

139

# Perfect puddings

There are some wonderfully decadent
creations in this section, and there is
a feast of fantastic names for this
fare too: you just know you'll enjoy
Boodles orange fool, whim wham,
Eton mess, Devonshire junket,
wardens in comfort, Sussex pond
pudding and Cumberland rum nicky.

# Gooseberry yogurt sorbet

Gooseberries from Cambridgeshire are available in June, July and August. Buy them fresh and use to make this delicious sorbet ready to enjoy in the garden on a warm summer's evening after dinner.

**Fresh or frozen gooseberries** 680g (1½lb), topped and tailed
**Granulated sugar** 110g (4oz)
**Gelatine** 1 sachet
**Natural yogurt** 275g (10oz)
**Egg whites** 2

1 Put the gooseberries and sugar in a saucepan with 4 tbsp water. Cover the pan and cook gently for around 10 minutes until the fruit is soft. Purée in a blender or food processor and then push through a nylon sieve. Leave to cool for 10 minutes.

2 Sprinkle the gelatine in 3 tbsp cold water in a small bowl and leave to soak for 3–4 minutes. Place the bowl in a saucepan of simmering water and stir, until the gelatine dissolves. Leave until lukewarm and then stir into the gooseberry purée. Add the yogurt and stir.

3 Whisk the egg whites until stiff but not dry and fold into the purée.

4 Pour the mixture into a rigid freezer container and freeze for about 3 hours or until almost frozen. Remove from the freezer and whisk well or blend in a food processor. Return to the freezer and freeze for at least 4 hours, until firm.

5 Before serving, transfer to the fridge for at least 30 minutes to soften.

## Cook's tip

• An uncooked gooseberry or two makes a pretty addition when serving the ice cream. Remember to reserve them before cooking the rest!

| | |
|---|---|
| Preparation time | 40 minutes plus freezing time |
| Calories per portion | 126 Kcal |
| Fat per portion | 1g |
| of which saturated | 0.3g |
| Serves | 6 |
| Suitable for freezing | |

# Atholl brose ice cream

Originally Atholl brose pudding didn't contain cream and was served as a drink. When cream was added it became a deliciously rich dessert, similar to a syllabub. Here the ingredients are frozen into an iced dessert.

**Eggs** 4 large, separated
**Caster sugar** 75g (3oz)
**Heather honey** 2 tbsp
**Double cream** 300ml (½ pint)
**Whisky** 4 tbsp
**Oatmeal** 4 tbsp, toasted
**Raspberries** to decorate

## Cook's tips

• You will find oatmeal with baking ingredients in the supermarket. Oatmeal is ground to different textures, and medium oatmeal is good for this recipe as it gives a little texture and oaty bite to the flavour. Use fine ground for a smoother texture.

• To freeze: label, seal well and store in the freezer for up to three months.

Preparation time – 15 minutes
Calories per portion – 382 Kcal
Fat per portion – 30g
of which saturated – 14g
Serves – 8
Suitable for vegetarians
Suitable for freezing

1 In a clean, dry bowl, whisk the egg whites until they form stiff peaks, and then gradually whisk in the sugar and honey until the mixture is thick and glossy – like meringue. Whisk in the egg yolks.

2 In a separate bowl, whip the cream until just peaking, and then fold into the egg mixture along with the whisky and oatmeal.

3 Transfer to a freezer-proof container and leave to freeze overnight. Stand at room temperature for 5–10 minutes before scooping and serving layered in tall glasses with fresh raspberries.

143

# Knickerbocker glory

This ice-cream extravaganza originated in New York and was named after its original Dutch settlers, the 'Knickerbockers'. However, its popularity here in Britain is due to an Italian, named Pacitto, who opened an ice-cream parlour in Redcar – where he introduced the Knickerbocker glory to the British.

**For the Melba sauce**
**Fresh raspberries** 250g (9oz)
**Caster sugar** 75g (3oz)
**Grand Marnier** 1 tbsp, optional

**For the fruit salad**
**Fresh pineapple** 175g (6oz) piece, prepared weight
**Pears** 2 small, peeled, cored and cut into small cubes
**Black small seedless grapes** 175g (6oz)
**Green small seedless grapes** 175g (6oz)
**Strawberries** 175g (6oz), hulled and quartered
**Peaches** 3 small, halved, stoned and skinned
**Cherries** 175g (6oz), pitted
**Caster sugar** 2–3 tbsp
**Lemon** 1, juice only

**For the chocolate sauce**
**Dark chocolate** 150g (5oz)
**Unsalted butter** 25g (1oz)

**For assembling**
**Vanilla ice cream** approximately 2 x 500ml tubs
**Ice cream wafers** 6
**Strawberries** 6
**Maraschino or fresh cherries** 6

1 To make the Melba sauce, put the raspberries, sugar and Grand Marnier (if using) into a bowl and mix together. Cover and leave to stand for 30 minutes, then pass the mixture through a fine nylon or stainless steel sieve to make a purée. Chill until required.

2 To prepare the fruit salad, cut away all the skin and 'eyes' from the pineapple, then cut into quarters and cut away the hard and woody centre core. Cut the flesh into small cubes and put into a large bowl.

3 Add all the remaining prepared fruits, sugar and lemon juice to the pineapple and mix well. If not using immediately, refrigerate until required.

4 Just before you are ready to assemble the Knickerbocker glory, make the chocolate sauce. Put the chocolate, butter and 150ml (¼ pint) cold water into a small saucepan and stir together over a moderate heat until the chocolate is melted and smoothly blended with the butter and water. Allow the sauce to cool until cold, but do not allow it to set.

5 To assemble the Knickerbocker glory, spoon a little of the Melba sauce into the bottom of each tall sundae glass (contains about 350ml/12fl oz), then add a little fruit salad, top with a scoop of ice cream and then pour on a little of the chocolate sauce.

6 Insert a wafer into each glass and decorate with strawberries and maraschino cherries. Serve immediately.

## Cook's tip

• Making this dessert from scratch can take rather a long time. However, if all of the vital components are prepared in advance, its final assembly can be speedily done in minutes!

| | |
|---|---|
| Preparation time | 45 minutes plus 15 minutes assembling |
| Calories per portion | 806 Kcal |
| Fat per portion | 49g |
| of which saturated | 24.1g |
| Serves | 6 |
| Suitable for vegetarians | |

145

# Boodle's orange fool

This dish is similar to trifle, with a sponge base that absorbs the delicious citrus juices. It originates from the Boodle's Club in St James's Street, London. Boodles, founded in the 18th century, was named after the club's original head waiter, who squandered his inheritance.

**Trifle sponges** 6, cut in half lengthways

**Oranges** 3 large, grated rind and juice of 2 plus segments of 1

**Lemon** 1, grated rind and juice

**Sugar** 25g (1oz)

**Double cream** 450ml (16fl oz)

**Orange and lemon rind curls** to decorate, optional

1 Place the sponge slices in a large serving bowl so that they cover the base and come halfway up the sides. Cover with the orange segments.

2 Mix the citrus rind and juice with the sugar, until it is completely dissolved.

3 Add the cream and whisk together until it is light and thickened.

4 Pour the mixture over the sponge and refrigerate overnight. Decorate with orange and lemon rind curls (if using) and serve.

## Cook's tips

• Take care not to over-whip the cream and juice mixture as it could separate.

• To make citrus fruit rind curls, use a zester, which neatly pares off the rind.

| | |
|---|---|
| Preparation time | 30 minutes plus chilling time |
| Calories per portion | 479 Kcal |
| Fat per portion | 41g |
| of which saturated | 22.7g |
| Serves | 6 |
| Suitable for vegetarians | |

# Whim wham

The word whimsy, meaning quaint or fanciful, originates from the phrase 'whim wham'. The words 'whim' and 'wham' were adopted by the Scots for this deliciously boozy, creamy and fruity trifle.

**Butter** 25g (1oz)
**Blanched almonds** 50g (2oz)
**Granulated sugar** 25g (1oz)
**Trifle sponge fingers** 75g (3oz)
**Sweet sherry** 150ml (¼ pint)
**Brandy** 4 tbsp
**Orange** 1, finely grated rind and juice
**Raspberries** 225g (8oz), optional, plus a few extra to decorate
**Double cream** 300ml (½ pint)
**Natural yogurt** 275g (10oz)

1 Melt the butter in a heavy-based frying pan and fry the almonds for 2–3 minutes until golden brown. Add the sugar and cook for 1 minute, stirring continuously, until the sugar dissolves and the almonds are coated. Leave to cool.

2 Around 30 minutes before you are ready to serve, break the sponge fingers in half and place in a serving bowl. Sprinkle the sherry, brandy and orange rind (reserving some for decoration) and juice over the sponges and leave to soak for 30 minutes. If using, top with raspberries.

3 Whip the cream until it holds soft peaks and then carefully fold in the yogurt. Spoon it over the sponge (and raspberries). Roughly chop the almonds, sprinkle on top with the remaining orange rind and raspberries and serve immediately.

## Cook's tip

• If you do not have sherry, use a dessert wine instead. You can also substitute orange segments for the raspberries and low-fat natural fromage frais for the yogurt.

| | |
|---|---|
| Preparation time | 10 minutes |
| Cooking time | 4 minutes |
| Calories per portion | 540 Kcal |
| Fat per portion | 36g |
| of which saturated | 18.2g |
| Serves | 6 |
| Suitable for vegetarians | |
| Suitable for freezing | |

# Eton mess

As its name would suggest, this dessert originates from Eton College in Berkshire, one of the most famous public schools in Britain. It is traditionally served at picnics following prize-giving ceremonies.

**Strawberries** 450g (1lb), hulled
**Cherry brandy** 4–5 tbsp
**Double cream** 300ml (½ pint)
**Small meringues** 6, crushed

1 Chop the strawberries, reserving a few for decoration, and place in a bowl. Sprinkle with the cherry brandy, cover and chill for 2 hours.

2 Whip the cream until it holds soft peaks. Gently fold in the chopped strawberries, juices and most of the crushed meringues. Spoon into serving dishes and decorate with the reserved strawberries and remaining meringue.

## Cook's tips

• You can use ordinary brandy or kirsch in place of the cherry brandy.
• For a healthier version, substitute low-fat strawberry yogurt for the cream, and omit the alcohol.

| | |
|---|---|
| Preparation time | 10 minutes plus 2 hours chilling |
| Calories per portion | 486 Kcal |
| Fat per portion | 40g |
| of which saturated | 22.6g |
| Serves | 4 |
| Suitable for vegetarians | |

148

# Devonshire junket

This is a simple dessert often served after a Sunday roast dinner or, as it's easily digestible, it's served to convalescents. If you're not counting calories, try serving it with clotted cream.

**Milk** 600ml (1 pint)
**Caster sugar** 2 tbsp
**Vegetarian rennet** ½ tsp
**Grated nutmeg** to decorate

1 Pour the milk into a saucepan and add the caster sugar. Warm it gently until it feels just luke warm to the touch.

2 Pour in the rennet and stir to mix it. Just before it sets, pour the milk into four dishes and leave it in a cool place to set.

3 Keep the junkets chilled until serving and just before serving grate nutmeg over the top.

## Cook's tip

• If the junket doesn't set then re-heat it to a slightly warmer temperature and let it set. If you like the junket to have more flavour, then you can add a few drops of vanilla extract.

| | |
|---|---|
| Preparation time | 5 minutes plus 20 minutes chilling time |
| Calories per portion | 101 Kcal |
| Fat per portion | 3g |
| of which saturated | 1.5g |
| Serves | 4 |
| Suitable for vegetarians | |

# Trinity College pudding

*Crème brulée* was introduced to Trinity College in Cambridge more than 100 years ago by one of its Fellows, a Scot from Aberdeen. It has become more commonly known as Trinity College pudding, or Cambridge cream. It requires patience but is worth the effort.

**Egg yolks** 6 large
**Caster sugar** 50g (2oz)
**Double cream** 750ml (1¼ pints)
**Vanilla beans** 2 or use 1 tsp vanilla essence
**Flameproof ramekin dishes** 6 x 150ml (¼ pint)

1 Place the egg yolks in a large mixing bowl, add 25g (1oz) of the sugar and whisk well until pale in colour and very thick.

2 Pour the cream into a saucepan, cut each vanilla bean lengthways, remove the curd from the centre and add it to the cream, along with the outer skin.

3 Gently heat the cream until hot, taking care not to let it boil, then whisk it into the egg yolks and sugar.

4 Place the bowl over a saucepan of gently boiling water and stir continuously until the mixture thickens enough to hold a light trail – do not be tempted to hurry the process (it can take up to an hour), as the mixture will curdle!

5 Remove and discard the outer skins of the vanilla beans, then pour the custard into the ramekin dishes. Place the ramekins on a large plate or small tray, allow the custards to cool, and then cover with cling film and refrigerate overnight.

6 The next day, preheat the grill until very hot. Sprinkle the remaining caster sugar evenly over the top of each custard, place the dishes in a grill pan or on a baking tray, then place under the grill for 1–2 minutes, just until the sugar melts and turns to a golden caramel colour.

7 Allow the caramel to cool and harden, then cover with foil or cling film and chill for at least 4–5 hours to re-set the custard.

## Cook's tips

• Provided they are well covered, the bruléed custards will keep well for two days in the refrigerator. The actual making of *crème brulée* is very simple – it just can't be hurried.
• Use the egg whites for making meringues, pavlova or macaroons.

| | |
|---|---|
| Preparation time | 1 hour 15 minutes, plus overnight and another 4–5 hours chilling time |
| Calories per portion | 727 Kcal |
| Fat per portion | 74g |
| Of which saturated | 39.5g |
| Serves | 6 |
| Suitable for vegetarians | |

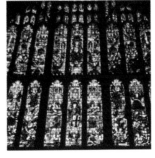

# Wardens in comfort

Old Warden in Bedfordshire is best known for its vintage aircraft museum and flying displays. However, it was once also well known for a variety of pear called Wardens – hence, when the pears were cooked in wine they acquired the title of 'wardens in comfort'.

**Red wine** 75cl bottle
**Soft light brown sugar** 110g (4oz)
**Clear honey** 110g (4oz)
**Orange** 1, finely pared rind and juice
**Lemon** 1, finely pared rind and juice
**Cinnamon stick** 7.5cm (3in) piece
**Pears** 8 medium–large Conference or Comice

1 Pour the wine into a large stainless steel saucepan. Add the sugar, honey, orange and lemon rinds and juice, and cinnamon and heat gently, stirring occasionally, until the sugar is dissolved.

2 Meanwhile, using a stainless steel vegetable peeler, remove the skin from the pears, leaving the stalks on. Remove the small calyx from the bottom of each pear with the tip of a knife. As each pear is prepared, place in the wine, basting it well all over.

3 Cook the pears gently in the wine for 25–30 minutes until they look translucent and the tip of a knife, when inserted into them, goes in easily. Turn and baste the pears occasionally with the wine. Transfer the pears to a serving bowl and set aside.

4 Bring the wine to the boil, then reduce the heat and allow it to boil gently until reduced, approximately by half, and syrupy.

5 Pour the wine over the pears and leave to cool. Then cover with cling film and refrigerate until serving. Serve with whipped double cream.

## Cook's tip

• Use any firm, ripe pear for this recipe. The pears can be eaten hot, but improve in flavour if left to steep in the wine for 1–2 days after cooking.

Preparation time – 30 minutes
Cooking time – 25–30 minutes
Calories per portion – 348 Kcal
Fat per portion – 1g
of which saturated – 0g
Serves – 4
Suitable for vegetarians
Suitable for freezing

152

# Baked apple and coconut

Here is a traditional fruit pudding, originating from Kent, where apple orchards once grew in abundance. Served hot with fresh creamy custard, this pudding is the perfect antidote to a rainy day.

**Muscovado sugar** 110g (4oz) plus 2 tbsp
**Lemon** 1, finely grated rind and juice
**Eating apples** 4, peeled, cored and sliced
**Butter** 110g (4oz)
**Eggs** 2, separated
**Self-raising flour** 110g (4oz)
**Baking powder** 1½ tsp
**Desiccated coconut** 25g (1oz) plus 1 tbsp
**Apricot jam** 4 tbsp, warmed

1 Preheat the oven to 170°C/325°F/Gas 3. Mix 2 tbsp of the sugar with the lemon juice in a large bowl. Add the apples and stir well.

2 Beat the remaining sugar with the butter until well blended. Add the lemon rind and then the egg yolks, one at a time, beating well. Stir in the flour, baking powder and coconut.

3 In a clean bowl, whisk the egg whites until stiff, then fold into the flour mixture. Spoon into a lightly greased 25cm (10in) flan dish. Press the apples into the mixture and spoon any juices over the top.

4 Place the dish on a baking tray and cook in the oven for 1–1¼ hours until well browned and firm. Cover with baking parchment, if necessary.

5 Cool for 15 minutes, then brush with the apricot jam and scatter with the tablespoon of desiccated coconut. Serve with custard.

## Cook's tip

• For this recipe try to use a British apple, such as Cox, as their taste and texture are perfect.

| | |
|---|---|
| Preparation time | 20 minutes |
| Cooking time | 1 hour 10 minutes |
| Calories per portion | 314 Kcal |
| Fat per portion | 16g |
| of which saturated | 10.1g |
| Serves | 8 |
| Suitable for vegetarians | |

# Raspberry sponge pudding

Although raspberries can be found growing everywhere in the British Isles, those that grow in northern parts are said to be sweeter. This whisky-flavoured pudding is topped with raspberries and served with a whisky-flavoured cream.

**Raspberry jam** 3 heaped tbsp
**Fresh raspberries** 300g (11oz)
**Unsalted butter** 175g (6oz)
**Soft light brown sugar** 75g (3oz)
**Caster sugar** 75g (3oz)
**Eggs** 3 large, beaten
**Scotch whisky** 4 tbsp
**Self–raising flour** 225g (8oz)
**Double cream** 300ml (½ pint)

1 Thoroughly grease a 2 litre (3½ pint) pudding basin with butter, then line the base with a greaseproof paper disc.

2 Spoon the jam into the bottom of the basin and spread evenly, then carefully arrange the raspberries in a single layer on top – allowing them to come slightly up the side of the bowl.

3 Beat together the butter, soft brown sugar and caster sugar until very light and fluffy, and then gradually beat in the eggs, and 2 tbsp of the whisky.

4 Fold the flour into the creamed mixture, carefully spoon it on top of the raspberries and spread evenly.

5 Cover the pudding basin with a sheet of foil, pleated in the middle, and secure with string. Steam the pudding for 1½–1¾ hours, until well risen and a skewer, when inserted into the centre, comes out clean.

6 While the pudding is cooking, whisk the remaining whisky with the double cream until it holds soft peaks – adding a teaspoon of caster sugar if wished. Spoon into a serving bowl, cover and refrigerate until serving.

7 Carefully un-mould the pudding onto a serving dish, garnish with mint leaves if wished, and serve hot accompanied with the whisky cream.

## Cook's tips

• This pudding does not rise to the top of the pudding basin, as it is intended to be wide and shallow, rather than traditional pudding basin shape.
• If you prefer your cream less rich, omit the whisky and sugar.

| | |
|---|---|
| Preparation time | 30 minutes |
| Cooking time | 1½-2 hours |
| Calories per portion | 612 Kcal |
| Fat per portion | 41g |
| of which saturated | 23.4g |
| Serves | 8 |
| Suitable for vegetarians | |

'Your wine it may do for
the bodies far south,
But a Scotsman likes something
that bites i' the mouth,
And whisky's the thing that
can do't to a tee.
Then Scotsmen and whisky
will ever agree.'
Alexander Rodger

PERFECT PUDDINGS

# Pinkerton pear sponge

In the late 18th century, Wigan was the home to one of the finest orchard nurseries in the country –William Pinkerton's. His 1782 catalogue offered 120 varieties of apple, 68 of pear and 48 of peach as well as 30 vines.

**Butter** 110g (4oz), softened, plus 1 tbsp
**Caster sugar** 110g (4oz)
**Eggs** 2
**Self-raising flour** 175g (6oz)
**Baking powder** ½ tsp
**Pears** 2 William or Conference

1 Preheat the oven to 180°C/350°F/Gas 4 and lightly butter a 20cm (8in) loose-based sandwich tin.

2 Cream together the butter and sugar in a bowl until light and fluffy. Beat in the eggs then sift and fold in the flour and baking powder. Spoon the mixture into the tin and smooth the top.

3 Peel, halve and core the pears and slice them thinly lengthways. Fan the slices out on top of the sponge mixture. Sprinkle with 1 tbsp of the extra sugar.

4 Bake in the middle of the oven for an hour, then 10–15 minutes longer if the sponge is not quite set in the middle. Remove from the oven and take out of the tin. Slice and serve warm with custard or cream or eat it cold.

## Cook's tips

• Use a melon baller to neatly take the core and seeds out of the pear halves.
• This looks best on the day it has been made but leftover sponge will keep for a few days. Warm slices through in the microwave for serving.

| | |
|---|---|
| Preparation time | 15 minutes |
| Cooking time | 1¼ hours |
| Calories per portion | 268 Kcal |
| Fat per portion | 13g |
| of which saturated | 7.6g |
| Serves | 8 |
| Suitable for vegetarians | |

# Monmouth pudding

'Pwdin mynwy' in Welsh, this simple light bread pudding is similar to the traditional English dessert, queen of puddings, but much lower in fat. It is named after the historic old town of Monmouth.

**White breadcrumbs** 225g (8oz)
**Milk** 300ml (½ pint)
**Granulated sugar** 4 tbsp
**Butter** 25g (1oz), cut into small pieces
**Nutmeg** ¼ tsp
**Eggs** 2 large, separated
**Raspberry jam** 6 tbsp

## Cook's tip

• For a zestier flavour, replace the nutmeg with approximately 1 tsp finely grated lemon rind.

| | |
|---|---|
| Preparation time | 15 minutes plus 10 minutes standing |
| Cooking time | 55 minutes |
| Calories per portion | 271 Kcal |
| Fat per portion | 5g |
| of which saturated | 2.7g |
| Serves | 6 |
| Suitable for vegetarians | |

**1** Preheat the oven to 180°C/350°F/Gas 4. Put the breadcrumbs in a heatproof bowl. Bring the milk to the boil and pour over the crumbs. Cover and leave to stand for 10 minutes.

**2** Break up with a fork and then work in 2 tbsp of the sugar together with the butter, nutmeg and egg yolks until well mixed. In another bowl, whisk the egg whites until stiff and fold into the bread mixture.

**3** Spoon 2 tbsp of the jam into the bottom of a greased 1.2 litre (2 pint) pudding basin and spoon over half the breadcrumb mixture. Spread the remaining jam over the top and add the remaining breadcrumb mixture. Cover with a layer of lightly greased foil and bake for about 50 minutes until set and firm to the touch.

**4** Preheat the grill to a hot setting. Sprinkle the remaining sugar over the top of the pudding and cook under the grill for about 5 minutes until caramelised, bubbling and golden. Serve warm with plenty of cream.

# Sussex pond pudding

This pudding was traditionally served on Palm Sunday. The long, slow cooking produces a rich, buttery centre that oozes out like a sauce. As it cooks, the lemon will soften – so when you cut into the pudding make sure everyone has a piece of the tangy rind.

**Self-raising flour** 225g (8oz)
**Shredded suet** 110g (4oz)
**Salt** pinch
**Water** 150ml (¼ pint)
**Butter** 110g (4oz), diced
**Light muscovado sugar** 110g (4oz)
**Lemon** 1 large, pricked all over with a fork

1 Tip the flour into a mixing bowl and stir in the suet and salt. Add the water and mix to a soft dough. Knead the dough lightly and roll it out on a floured surface to make a large circle. Cut out a quarter of the dough circle and use the remaining piece to line the pudding basin. Reserve the smaller piece for the lid.

2 Put half the butter and half the sugar into the basin and place the lemon on top. Then add the remaining butter and sugar. Re-roll the reserved pastry for the top. Brush water around the edge of the pastry lining the bowl, place the lid on top and press the edges well to seal them. Cover the basin with a double layer of baking parchment with a pleat in it, to allow for the expansion of the pudding during cooking.

3 Place the basin on a trivet in a large saucepan and pour boiling water in to come about halfway up the sides of the basin. Cover the pan and boil for 3½–4 hours, checking the water level regularly to ensure it doesn't boil dry.

4 Remove the basin from the saucepan and uncover the bowl. Ease the pudding away from the basin using a palette knife and then turn it carefully out onto a serving dish.

## Cook's tip

• Serve the pudding on a dish with a rim as a rich, buttery sauce will pour out when the pudding is cut.

| | |
|---|---|
| Preparation time | 15 minutes |
| Cooking time | 3½–4 hours |
| Calories per portion | 484 Kcal |
| Fat per portion | 31g |
| of which saturated | 17g |
| Serves | 6 |
| | Suitable for freezing |

# Damson and apple tansy

A tansy would originally have contained the bitter-sweet herb tansy, which still gives its name to many custard and omelette-type dishes. This recipe would traditionally have used Witherslack damsons, which grow south of Lake Windermere.

**Cox apples** 2 large, peeled, cored and thinly sliced

**Damsons** 225g (8oz), halved, stoned and quartered

**Butter** 15g (½oz)

**Sugar** 40g (1½oz)

**Ground cloves** ½ tsp

**Ground cinnamon** ½ tsp

**Eggs** 4, separated

**Soured cream** 142ml tub

1 Put the apples, damsons, butter and half of the sugar in a large frying pan. Cook over a low heat until the fruit is softened, stirring continuously. Add the cloves and cinnamon. Stir well and remove from the heat.

2 Beat the egg yolks with the soured cream and whisk the egg whites until stiff and carefully fold into the yolks and cream. Then stir in the fruit and return everything to the pan.

3 Cook over a low heat until the mixture has set. Then sprinkle with the remaining sugar and brown under a hot grill. Serve immediately, with soured cream or natural yogurt.

## Cook's tips

• If it is the wrong time of year for damsons, use plums instead.

• If your frying pan has a plastic handle, take care when browning under the grill.

| | |
|---|---|
| Preparation time | 10 minutes |
| Cooking time | 10 minutes |
| Calories per portion | 289 Kcal |
| Fat per portion | 17g |
| of which saturated | 8.2g |
| Serves | 4 |
| Suitable for vegetarians | |

# Kentish pudding pie

Also known as Kent Lent pie this pudding was devised as a treat for those observing Lent and was particularly popular in Folkstone. It is similar to a cheesecake but as it doesn't contain gelatine, it's suitable for vegetarians.

**Plain wholemeal flour** 175g (6oz)
**Salt** pinch
**Butter** 150g (5oz)
**Ground rice** 25g (1oz)
**Milk** 300ml (½ pint)
**Sugar** 50g (2oz)
**Eggs** 2
**Lemon** 1, finely grated rind
**Grated nutmeg** ¼ tsp
**Currants** 25g (1oz)

## Cook's tip

• To bake blind, prick the base of the tart with a fork. Line with a large piece of greaseproof paper and baking beans (or dried pasta). Bake for 10 minutes, remove paper and baking beans (or pasta) and cook for 5 more minutes until the pastry case is just cooked.

Preparation time – 20 minutes
Cooking time – 1 hour
Calories per portion – 583 Kcal
Fat per portion – 37g
of which saturated – 21.3g
Serves – 4
Suitable for vegetarians

1 Preheat the oven to 200°C/400°F/Gas 6. Put the flour and salt in a bowl and rub in 75g (3oz) of the butter and mix until the mixture resembles fine breadcrumbs. Add about 2 tbsp water and mix to a smooth dough.

2 Roll out the pastry onto a floured surface and use to line a greased 30cm (8in) fluted flan dish or tin. Bake blind (see Cook's tip) for 10–15 minutes, until set.

3 Meanwhile, put the rice into a saucepan and add the milk. Bring to the boil, stirring continuously, until the mixture thickens. Remove from the heat and leave to cool.

4 Cream together the remaining butter and sugar until pale and fluffy. Beat in the eggs, one at a time, then add the lemon rind, nutmeg and the cold rice. Add a little salt. Mix thoroughly and pour into the flan case. Sprinkle the currants on the top.

5 Reduce the oven temperature to 190°C/375°F/Gas 5 and bake for 40–45 minutes, until firm to the touch and golden brown. Serve warm.

# Greengage tart

More than 200 years ago Sir William Gage planted some plum trees at Hengrave Hall near Bury St Edmunds. The plums turned out to be green and became known as the green Gage's plum. This was later simply shortened to greengage.

**Plain wholemeal flour** 175g (6oz)

**Salt** ¼ tsp

**Butter** 75g (3oz)

**Hazelnuts** 25g (1oz), toasted and finely chopped

**Soft light brown sugar** 1 tbsp

**Eggs** 3 large

**Greengages or plums** 450g (1lb), halved and stoned

**Single cream** 300ml (½ pint)

**Caster sugar** 25g (1oz)

1 Preheat the oven to 200°C/400°F/Gas 6. To make the pastry, put the flour and salt in a bowl and rub in the butter until the mixture resembles fine breadcrumbs. Add the hazelnuts, sugar and 1 beaten egg. Mix together to form a soft but not sticky dough.

2 Knead the dough on a lightly floured surface, then roll out and use to line a greased 25cm (10in) fluted flan tin. Line the flan tin with a crumpled square of baking paper and sprinkle a layer of baking beans or rice in the bottom. Bake blind for 10 minutes until set and then remove the beans or rice.

3 Arrange the fruit, cut side down, in the pastry case. Beat the remaining eggs with the cream and sugar and pour over the fruit. Bake for 30–40 minutes, until golden and puffy, and serve while it is warm.

## Cook's tip

• In season towards the end of August, greengages are delicious in this nutty tart. Use plums at other times of year.

| | |
|---|---|
| Preparation time | 40 minutes |
| Cooking time | 30–40 minutes |
| Calories per portion | 417 Kcal |
| Fat per portion | 27g |
| of which saturated | 13.7g |
| Serves | 6 |
| Suitable for vegetarians | |
| Suitable for freezing | |

# Blueberry crumble

In 1946, as a thank you for what we had gone through in the war, the British Columbia University Berry Farm on Lulu Island in Canada offered a box of 80 blueberry plants free to any grower in Britain. David Trehane of James Trehane and Sons Limited, nurserymen near Wimborne, Dorset, took up the offer and the bushes flourished.

**Blueberries** 450g (1lb)
**Caster sugar** 150g (5oz)
**Lemon** 1, grated rind and juice
**Breadcrumbs** 75g (3oz)
**Ground almonds** 75g (3oz)
**Butter** 110g (4oz)
**Slivered or flaked almonds** 25g (1oz)

1 Preheat the oven to 200°C/400°F/Gas 6. Mix the fruit, 75g (3oz) of the sugar and lemon rind and juice in a shallow ovenproof dish.

2 Make the crumble by mixing the breadcrumbs, ground almonds and remaining sugar. Rub in, or cut in, the butter roughly and spoon the mixture evenly over the fruit. Scatter with slivered or flaked almonds.

3 Bake the crumble for about 30 minutes, turning the oven heat down to 180°C/350°F/Gas 4 after 15 minutes when the top has browned. Serve warm or cold with plenty of cream – clotted or double!

## Cook's tips

• Crumbles are pretty flexible with the cooking temperature they need. If you're cooking other things in the oven at the same time, the crumble will cope – just cook it until it looks good.
• Breadcrumbs give a crisper top than the usual flour crumble mixture.

| | |
|---|---|
| Preparation time | 15 minutes |
| Cooking time | 30 minutes |
| Calories per portion | 388 Kcal |
| Fat per portion | 25g |
| of which saturated | 10.2g |
| Serves | 6 |
| Suitable for vegetarians | |

'Sweeter than the odours borne on southern gales, Comes the clotted nectar of my native vales – Crimped and golden crusted, rich beyond compare, Food on which a goddess evermore would fare.'

Edward Capern

# Ripe tart

The name of this dish comes from the village of Ripe in Sussex, where a pie feast celebrated the cherry harvest. Ripe was owned by Earl Harold, later to become the King Harold who was killed at the Battle of Hastings in 1066.

**Plain flour** 175g (6oz)

**Salt** pinch

**Cornflour** 25g (1oz)

**Icing sugar** 110g (4oz) plus 2 tsp and a little for decorating

**Butter** 75g (3oz)

**Eggs** 2 plus 1 yolk

**Cherries** 450g (1lb), stoned

**Ground almonds** 75g (3oz)

**Almond essence** few drops

**Flaked almonds** 25g (1oz)

### Cook's tip

• Try this flan with plums or apricots, for a change.

| | |
|---|---|
| Preparation time | 25 minutes |
| Cooking time | 1 hour 15 minutes |
| Calories per portion | 330 Kcal |
| Fat per portion | 16g |
| of which saturated | 6g |
| Serves | 8 |
| Suitable for vegetarians | |

1 Sift the flour, salt, cornflour and 2 tsp of the icing sugar into a bowl. Rub in the butter until it resembles fine breadcrumbs.

2 Add the egg yolk and a little water to bind together. Knead lightly on a floured surface and roll out. Place a 23cm (9in) diameter loose-bottomed fluted flan ring on a baking tray and line with the pastry. Preheat the oven to 200°C/400°F/Gas 6 and chill the flan case while the oven warms up.

3 Bake the pastry case blind for 15 minutes (see Cook's tip on page 160). Remove baking beans and cook for 5 minutes more. Turn down the oven to 170°C/325°F/Gas 3.

4 Arrange the cherries in the flan case. Mix the icing sugar, eggs, almonds and essence and pour over. Bake in the oven for 50–60 minutes, until the top is firm and golden. Halfway through cooking, sprinkle flaked almonds over the top. Serve hot or cold dusted with sifted icing sugar and with pouring cream.

# Bakewell tart

Formerly know as Bakewell pudding, this tart was apparently created by a cook working at the Rutland Arms Hotel, Bakewell. The cook was making jam tarts but used puff pastry by mistake, so he decided to use up some leftover ingredients, creating this delicious dish.

**Puff pastry** 250g (9oz), thawed if frozen
**Raspberry jam** 75g (3oz)
**Ground almonds** 110g (4oz)
**Caster sugar** 110g (4oz)
**Butter** 50g (2oz), softened
**Eggs** 3, beaten
**Almond essence** ¼ tsp

1 Preheat the oven to 200°C/400°F/Gas 6 and place a baking tray in the oven. On a lightly floured surface, roll the pastry into a square large enough to line a buttered 900ml (1½ pint) shallow pie dish.

2 Transfer the pastry to the pie dish and trim off any excess. Knock up the pastry edge with a knife so the pastry layers rise well during baking. Brush the base of the pastry case with the jam and chill while making the filling.

3 In a large bowl, beat the almonds with the sugar, butter, eggs and almond essence. Remove the case from the fridge and spoon the mixture on top of the jam. Smooth the top.

4 Place the tart on the hot baking tray and bake in the oven for 30–35 minutes, until the filling has set. Serve hot with custard or cold with cream.

## Cook's tip

• Today's commercial Bakewell tarts are quite different, with a sweet pastry base and the top covered with a deep layer of white icing.

| | |
|---|---|
| Preparation time | 30 minutes |
| Cooking time | 30–35 minutes |
| Calories per portion | 480 Kcal |
| Fat per portion | 30g |
| of which saturated | 9.9g |
| Serves | 6 |
| Suitable for vegetarians | |
| Suitable for freezing | |

# Cumberland rum nicky

The ports of Whitehaven, Workington and Maryport were at the centre of the UK rum trade in the 18th century, importing rum, molasses and sugar from the Caribbean. The Cumbrians combined these imported ingredients to create this delicious dessert.

**Stoned dates** 225g (8oz), chopped
**Ready-to-eat dried apricots** 110g (4oz), chopped
**Chopped glacé ginger** 50g (2oz)
**Light rum** 3 tbsp
**Orange** 1, juice only
**Soft light brown sugar** 2 tbsp
**Plain flour** 225g (8oz)
**Salt** pinch
**Butter** 130g (4½oz)
**Egg yolk** 1, lightly beaten
**Milk** 1 tbsp
**Demerara sugar** to decorate

1 Preheat the oven to 200°C/400°F/Gas 6. Mix the dates, apricots, ginger, rum and orange juice together with half of the sugar. Leave to soak while making the pastry.

2 Put the flour and salt in a bowl and add 110g (4oz) of the butter. Rub in until the mixture resembles fine breadcrumbs. Add the remaining sugar and then the egg yolk and about 2 tbsp water to bind together.

3 Knead the pastry lightly on a floured surface. Roll out half of the pastry and use to line a greased 25cm (10in) flat pie plate.

4 Spread the fruit mixture over the pastry and dot with the remaining butter. Brush the edge with a little water.

5 Roll out the remaining pastry and use to cover the pie. Make a hole in the centre to allow steam to escape. If you have any pastry left over, use it to form leaves with which to decorate the top of the pie. Brush with milk and bake for 30–35 minutes. Sprinkle with demerara sugar and serve hot with cream.

## Cook's tips

• For a shiny pie top, brush the pastry with beaten egg instead of milk.
• If you don't have a pie plate, look out for an ovenproof, deepish plate with a wide rim.

| | |
|---|---|
| Preparation time | 15 minutes |
| Cooking time | 35 minutes |
| Calories per portion | 499 Kcal |
| Fat per portion | 20g |
| Of which saturated | 11.7g |
| Serves | 6 |
| Suitable for vegetarians | |
| Suitable for freezing | |

# Banbury apple pie

The nursery rhyme 'Ride a Cock Horse' made Banbury one of England's best known towns. While the 'fine lady' is popularly said to have been Lady Godiva, historians believe she was a local girl who rode in a May Day procession. Banbury is also well known for its apple pie.

**Plain flour** 350g (12oz)

**Salt** ½ tsp

**Unsalted butter** 175g (6oz)

**Caster sugar** 1 tbsp plus extra for sprinkling

**Egg** 1, lightly beaten

**Cooking apples** 450g (1lb)

**Lemon** 1, grated rind and juice

**Sultanas** 50g (2oz)

**Soft light brown sugar** 50g (2oz)

**Ground cinnamon** ½ tsp

**Grated nutmeg** ¼ tsp

**Cornflour** 1 tbsp

**Milk** to glaze

## Cook's tips

• If you find that your pie is browning too quickly, cover with foil during cooking.

• To freeze, do not sprinkle with sugar, but allow to cool before wrapping in foil. Thaw in the fridge overnight and serve cold or warm in the oven for 20–25 minutes at 180°C/350°F/Gas 4.

Preparation time – 20 minutes
Cooking time – 40 minutes
Calories per portion – 543 Kcal
Fat per portion – 26g
of which saturated – 15.6g
Serves – 6
Suitable for vegetarians
Suitable for freezing

1 Preheat the oven to 200°C/400°F/Gas 6. In a bowl, mix the flour and salt and rub in the butter until the mixture resembles fine breadcrumbs. Add the caster sugar and then the egg and mix well. Add enough water to bind the mixture together.

2 Knead lightly on a floured surface and then roll out two-thirds of the pastry and use to line a 900ml (1½ pint) pie plate or tart tin. Brush the edge with water.

3 Peel, core and slice the apples and sprinkle with lemon juice. Mix the apples, sultanas, brown sugar, spices and cornflour and spoon into the pie dish.

4 Roll out the remaining pastry for the lid of the pie, reserving some for decoration, and press together the edges. Mark the edges with a fork and make a slit in the centre. With the remaining pastry, cut out leaves and 'stick' on the lid with milk.

5 Brush the top of the pie with milk and bake in the oven for 40 minutes, until golden brown (covering the top with foil, if necessary). Sprinkle with caster sugar and serve hot or cold.

SAY CHEESE

# Cheeseboard

A cheese course can be part of a sophisticated supper or a delightful snack in its own right. With the dessert finished, this is a time when everyone, including the host, can simply relax and enjoy this fine fare, accompanied by crackers, grapes and perhaps port.

Here in Britain, we are blessed with a wealth of different, high quality cheeses. Cheddar is still the top-selling cheese, with a market share of 67 per cent. Although a good Cheddar is delicious, why not try some of our more unusual cheeses? They will make your cheeseboard look more interesting and give your taste buds a treat too!

On this page we have made a few suggestions for lesser-known cheeses from around Britain. Give them a try or visit your local cheese shop and choose a cheese made by producers in your locality. Some of these cheeses are unpasteurised (we have stated which). We wouldn't recommend these to expectant mothers, young children or the elderly.

**From front to back**

### Yorkshire Blue

Made by Shepherd's Purse in North Yorkshire, this ewes' milk cheese uses traditional methods dating back to the eleventh century. It was introduced in 1995 and won a British Cheese Award gold medal in 1997. Yorkshire Blue is a creamy, tangy cheese.

### Ribblesdale

A farmhouse hard goats' cheese with a smooth rind covered with a green wax. Created in Ribblesdale, Yorkshire in 1982, this cheese has a fresh, delicate flavour. The texture is rather like a young Gouda. This cheese won a bronze medal at the 1996 British Cheese Awards.

### Bowland

A crumbly Lancashire cheese with apple, raisin and cinnamon, which tastes like Christmas pudding! This is a great dessert cheese, created by David Williams, whose shop is in the cobbled square of the small market town of Sandbach, in Cheshire.

### Cheddar and farmhouse pickle

Also made by David Williams, this tangy cheese won a gold award at the 2005 Nantwich Cheese Show.

**From front to back**

### Caboc

Caboc is Scotland's oldest cheese, created in the fifteenth century in the western Highlands. The cheese was first made by the daughter of a chieftain – when under threat from a rival clan the chieftan's daughter escaped to Ireland where she learned how to make cheese. She brought her cheese knowledge back to Scotland and created Caboc. The recipe, still kept secret, has been handed down from mother to daughter ever since and is presently made by Highland Fine Cheeses Ltd. Each cheese, made from double cream, is rolled in toasted pinhead oatmeal.

### Laverbread

This cheese is a combination of Llanboidy, from rare Red Poll cows, and seaweed. Laverbread is made from a specific type of seaweed that grows on the shoreline in various places around the British coast. The seaweed is gathered from the rocks at low tide and then either dried or tinned. Although laverbread has been made in Ireland and Scotland in the past, its production is now restricted to a certain part of South Wales. With its speckled texture and mature flavour, Laverbread unpasteurised cheese makes an interesting addition to any cheeseboard.

### Smoked Cilowen organic

As a bronze winner at the World Cheese Awards, Cilowen Organic must be pretty special. This version is naturally smoked over oak logs, and has a smooth texture with a strong, smoky tang.

169

**From front to back**

### Sage Derby

Made by Belton Farm in Shropshire this Sage Derby is a green-veined cheese with a mild sage flavour. It was originally only made for festive occasions such as the harvest and Christmas but now it is made all year round. Its unusual colouring makes it an interesting addition to your cheeseboard.

### Dovedale

This relatively new soft blue cheese is simply delicious. It is produced by Hartington Creamery in the Peak District.

The creamery was originally established by the Duke of Devonshire, and was awarded the royal warrant to supply Stilton to King George V. It now produces about one quarter of the world's supply of Blue Stilton as well as lesser-known cheeses such as Dovedale.

### Shropshire Blue

This cheese has a misleading name as it has nothing to do with the county of Shropshire. In fact, it originated in Scotland in the 1970s, before its production was transferred to Leicestershire. This crumbly yet creamy cheese has a sharp flavour.

### Staffordshire Organic with chive

Bronze medal winning Staffordshire Organic cheese was originally made by Betty Deaville of New House Farm in Staffordshire, for her family. In the mid-1970s, the farm converted to organic, and Betty started making cheese with the farm's milk. At that time, organic cheese was almost impossible to buy. Betty's cheese was so popular among her friends that she decided to go into business. Staffordshire Organic is a hard, unpasteurised cows' cheese with a sweet, summery tang and a wonderfully smooth texture.

**From back to front**

## Cornish Yarg
This cheese is a light, creamy, mould-ripened cheese whose unique character and taste result from being wrapped in nettle leaves. This traditional method of coating cheese survives only in Cornish Yarg and gives it a distinctive pattern. The cheese was named Yarg – Gray spelt backwards after Alan Gray, the founder of Lynher Valley Dairy, where the cheese is produced.

## Tornegus
James Aldridge creates this cheese from Duckett's Caerphilly marinated in herbs, brine and wine from Kent. It is matured for ten weeks and acquires a strong flavour. This unpasteurised cheese may require the use of a nose peg!

## Waterloo
The rich Guernsey milk used in this cheese results in a golden, custardy paste with an earthy flavour. A 2003 gold medal winner, this unpasteurised cheese is delicious.

# Feasts and festivals

Tradition helps us decide what to eat for many celebrations: roast turkey at Christmas followed by Christmas pudding; Simnel cake at Easter. There are also national dishes such as the Scottish Burns' Night supper of haggis, neeps and tatties, Welsh lamb and English roast beef.

Burns' Night

# Haggis, neeps and tatties

On 25 January, the Scots celebrate the birth of their national poet, Robbie Burns, with this traditional meal. The platter of haggis is piped into the room of assembled diners, and then the 'Ode to the Haggis' is recited as the haggis is 'slashed' open and served.

**Haggis** 680g (1½lb)

**Turnip or swede** 1, peeled and cut into small chunks

**Salt and freshly ground black pepper**

**Maris Piper potatoes** 450g (1lb), peeled and cut into small chunks

**Butter** 50g (2oz)

**Warm milk** 3 tbsp

**Snipped chives** for garnishing

1 Cook the haggis according to the manufacturer's instructions. As a rough guide, remove any plastic covering, but leave the haggis 'skin' intact. Wrap it in foil and place in a saucepan. Cover with boiling water and gently poach, without boiling, for about an hour.

2 Meanwhile, place the turnip or swede in a saucepan, cover with water and add a pinch of salt. Bring to the boil and cook for about 15 minutes until tender. Drain and return to the pan.

3 Place the potatoes in another saucepan and cover with water. Add a pinch of salt, bring to the boil and cook for 15 minutes until tender. Drain well and return to the pan.

4 Mash the swede and potatoes well using a potato masher and add 25g (1oz) of the butter to each. Mix and season with black pepper and more salt if required. Stir the milk into the potato. Pile into warm dishes, cover and keep warm until required.

5 To serve, place the haggis on a warm platter. Remove the skin before scooping onto serving plates and accompanying with the mashed 'neeps' and 'tatties', sprinkled with snipped chives. It is delicious served with redcurrant or other fruit jelly.

## Cook's tips

• If you're vegetarian, there are veggie haggis as well, made from breadcrumbs, grated vegetables and chopped nuts, flavoured with herbs and spices.

• Serve Cock-a-leekie soup (page 31) as a starter to this main meal.

| | |
|---|---|
| Preparation time | 20 minutes |
| Cooking time | 1½ hours |
| Calories per portion | 750 Kcal |
| Fat per portion | 48g |
| of which saturated | 28.8g |
| Serves | 4 |

Shrove Tuesday

# Apple and raspberry pancakes

Olney in Buckinghamshire is famous for its annual pancake race for housewives – where the winner's prize is a prayer book and a kiss from the vicar. Traditionally, pancakes are served simply, sprinkled with lemon juice and sugar – this is a rather more special version.

**Plain flour** 110g (4oz)
**Salt** pinch
**Egg** 1 large
**Milk** 300ml (½ pint)
**Unsalted butter** 50g (2oz), melted and cooled, plus extra for cooking
**Cooking apples** 500g (1lb 2oz), peeled, cored and sliced
**Lemon** 1, strained juice only
**Granulated sugar** 110g (4oz)
**Fresh raspberries** 250g (9oz)
**Soft light brown sugar** 25g (1oz)
**Juice from cooked apples** 3 tbsp

**1** To make the batter, sift the flour and salt into a bowl and make a well in the centre. Break the egg into the flour and whisk it into the flour – adding the milk as the mixture thickens. Whisk in 25g (1oz) of the melted butter, cover and leave to stand.

**2** To make the filling, place the apples, lemon juice and sugar in a saucepan, cover and cook until the apples are soft and fluffy. Pour into a sieve placed over a bowl and leave to drain and cool.

**3** To cook the pancakes, heat a 20cm (8in) pancake pan or frying pan until hot, then grease with butter. Take a ladleful of the batter and pour it into the pan, quickly swirl over the bottom until evenly coated, then pour excess back into the bowl.

**4** Cook the pancake until it appears dry on the surface and is lightly browned underneath. Then 'flip' it or turn it over with a palette knife. Brown the other side, turn out onto a large plate and cover with a sheet of kitchen paper. Make seven more pancakes in the same way interleaving each with kitchen paper.

**5** Preheat the oven to 220°C/425°F/Gas 7. Place one of the pancakes on a flat surface and spoon an eighth of the apples and raspberries, reserving some for decoration, into the centre and close to the edge nearest to you. Bring the sides in and over the filling, then roll up and return to the pan (if it has a metal handle) or a well-buttered ovenproof dish. Repeat with remaining pancakes. Drizzle over rest of melted butter, and sprinkle with sugar and 3 tbsp of the reserved apple juice.

**6** Bake in the oven for 10–15 minutes until the sugar dissolves and is lightly browned. Decorate with reserved raspberries. Serve immediately.

## Cook's tips

• The method described here for cooking pancakes makes thin, light and delicate ones that are not stodgy.
• Pancakes can be prepared several hours before filling – interleaved with non-stick baking paper, then covered with cling film or foil and refrigerated. They can also be frozen.
• Chill the remaining apple juice and serve diluted with sparkling mineral water as a refreshing drink.

| | |
|---|---|
| Preparation time | 30 minutes |
| Cooking time | 10–15 minutes |
| Calories per portion | 458 Kcal |
| Fat per portion | 19g |
| of which saturated | 11g |
| Serves | 4 |
| Suitable for vegetarians | |

Good Friday

# Fish pie

Lent is the traditional season of renewal and repentance in Christ. The Church prescribes that Ash Wednesday and Good Friday are to be observed as days of abstinence. Abstinence always meant the giving up of meat and so many people would often eat fish instead.

**Milk** 450ml (16fl oz)

**Smoked haddock** 350g (12oz)

**King prawns** 175g (6oz), defrosted if frozen

**Butter** 50g (2oz)

**Leek** 1, washed and sliced

**Mushrooms** 150g (5oz), halved if large

**Plain flour** 2 tbsp

**Double cream** 150ml (¼ pint)

**Dill** 2 tbsp

**Salt and freshly ground black pepper**

**Ready-rolled puff pastry** 375g packet

**Egg** 1, lightly beaten, for glaze

1 Pour the milk into a saucepan and add the haddock. Bring to the boil and cook the fish for 4–5 minutes, until the fish is cooked through. Strain the fish, reserving the cooking liquor. Remove any skin from the haddock and break the fish into large pieces and place in the base of a 1.25 litre (2 pint) pie dish and arrange the prawns on top.

2 Melt half the butter in a large pan and add the leek and mushrooms and cook them over a moderate heat for about 5 minutes, until the leek has softened. Spoon the vegetables out of the pan and place them on top of the fish, keeping the cooking juices in the pan.

3 Add the remaining butter to the pan and place it over a gentle heat until it's melted. Add the flour to the pan, stirring well until it binds together. Gradually add the fish cooking liquor, stirring well between each addition of liquid to give a smooth sauce.

4 Simmer the sauce for 1–2 minutes, then add the cream. Simmer until it thickens slightly, then stir in the dill and season it to taste. Pour the sauce over the fish, and leave it to cool slightly.

5 Preheat the oven to 220°C/425°F/Gas 7. Unroll the pastry, and roll it slightly bigger if necessary so it's large enough to cover the pie dish. Cut narrow strips off the edge of the pastry. Dampen the edge of the pie dish with water and stick a single layer of the strips around the edge.

6 Use a sharp knife to score a criss-cross pattern through the main pastry sheet. Dampen the pastry strips with water and lift the main pastry sheet over the pie. Press the edges well to seal them. Trim off the excess around the edge of the dish, re-roll and cut out some small fish shapes to decorate the top. Use a knife to knock up the edges. Brush the top of the pastry with egg glaze. Make a couple of holes in the pastry in the centre to allow the steam to escape during cooking.

7 Bake the pie in the centre of the oven for 15 minutes, then reduce the temperature to 180°C/350°F/Gas 4 and cook the pie for a further 15–20 minutes until the pastry is an even golden colour and the filling is bubbling. Serve immediately with steamed cabbage or carrots.

## Cook's tip

• To get a really even glaze, the egg may be put through a tea-strainer to remove any stringy bits.

| | |
|---|---|
| Preparation time | 25 minutes |
| Cooking time | 50 minutes |
| Calories per portion | 844 Kcal |
| Fat per portion | 56g |
| of which saturated | 28.1g |
| Serves | 4 |

177

Easter
# Simnel cake

One of the oldest Christian festivals, Easter marks Christ's resurrection from the dead. Simnel cake has at some point been adopted as a traditional Easter cake. The 11 marzipan balls on the top represent the apostles, minus the treacherous Judas.

**Butter** 250g (9oz), softened
**Light muscovado sugar** 250g (9oz)
**Eggs** 4
**Plain flour** 300g (11oz)
**Baking powder** 1 tsp
**Ground mixed spice** 2 tsp
**Ground almonds** 50g (2oz)
**Luxury dried mixed fruit** 500g (1lb 2oz)
**Lemon** 1, finely grated zest and 2 tbsp juice
**White marzipan** 500g (1lb 2oz)
**Apricot glaze or sieved apricot jam** 2 tbsp

1 Preheat the oven to 150°C/300°F/Gas 2 and line a 20cm (8in) cake tin with baking parchment.

2 Cream together the butter and sugar until light and fluffy. Beat in the eggs one at a time, adding a spoonful of the flour along with each egg. Sift in the remaining flour, baking powder and spice and fold the almonds, dried fruit and lemon zest and juice into the mixture. Spoon half into the cake tin and smooth the surface level.

3 Roll out one third of the marzipan until it's a circle, just smaller than the cake tin, and lay it on top of the mixture in the tin. Spoon the remaining mixture over the top and level the surface.

4 Bake the cake in the centre of the oven for 2–2¼ hours, or until a skewer comes out clean after being inserted into the cake. Cover with a sheet of baking parchment if it starts to brown. When cooked, remove the cake from the oven and leave to cool.

5 Remove the cake from the tin and peel away the lining paper. Spread the apricot glaze or jam over the top. Roll out half of the remaining marzipan to fit the top of the cake. Place it on the cake and smooth down, taking care not to trap any air pockets underneath. Pinch around the edges.

6 Divide the remaining marzipan into 11 pieces and roll each into a ball. Brush a little apricot glaze or jam onto the base of each and evenly space around the top of the cake. Place under a hot grill to brown the marzipan lightly. Remove from the grill and leave to cool before serving.

## Cook's tips

• The cake will keep in an airtight container for up to a week.
• If you have a choice of marzipan, choose white marzipan, which has a more natural flavour than golden marzipan.

| | |
|---|---|
| Preparation time | 30 minutes |
| Cooking time | 2¼ hours |
| Calories per slice | 722 Kcal |
| Fat per slice | 30g |
| of which saturated | 13.2g |
| Makes | 11 slices |
| Suitable for vegetarians | |

St David's Day

# Roast leg of Welsh lamb

Dewi Sant, or Saint David, was a Celtic monk who lived in the 6th century. He was one of the early saints who helped to spread Christianity among the pagan tribes of western Britain. Celebrate St David's Day on 1 March with traditional roast lamb.

**Leg of Welsh lamb** 2.2kg (4lb 12oz), at room temperature

**Rosemary** 15–20 small sprigs plus extra for garnishing

**Olive oil** 1–2 tbsp

**Salt and freshly ground black pepper**

**Mint leaves** 50g (2oz)

**Caster sugar** 1½ tbsp

**Boiling water** 3 tbsp

**White or red wine vinegar** 150ml (¼ pint)

**Plain flour** 2 tbsp

**Red or white wine** 150ml (¼ pint)

**Lamb or chicken stock** 300ml (½ pint)

1 Preheat the oven to 220°C/425°F/Gas 7. Wipe the lamb all over with kitchen paper and then, with a small, sharp, pointed knife, make 15–20 small incisions all over the leg. Insert a small sprig of rosemary into each incision. Place the lamb on a roasting rack in a roasting tin, drizzle with olive oil and sprinkle with salt.

2 Cook the lamb in the centre of the oven for 20 minutes, then reduce the temperature to 180°C/350°F/Gas 4, and, for lamb that is slightly pink, continue cooking for another 1 hour 10 minutes. For well-done lamb, continue cooking for another 10 minutes – taking care not to overcook, as the meat will lose its succulence.

3 While the lamb is cooking, make the mint sauce – about 20 minutes before the lamb is due to be ready. Place the mint leaves on a chopping board, sprinkle with the sugar and then chop finely. Place in a bowl and stir in the hot water. Stir the vinegar into the mint, then pour into a serving jug or bowl.

4 Carefully remove the leg of lamb from the rack, place it on a serving dish, loosely cover with foil and set aside while making the gravy.

5 To make the gravy, pour all the cooking juices into a bowl, and then skim off all the fat from the surface.

6 Pour 2–3 tbsp of the lamb fat into the roasting tin and stir in the flour, then add the cooking juices, wine and stock. Place the roasting tin over a moderate heat and bring the mixture to the boil, stirring and scraping any browned residue from the bottom of the tin.

7 Allow the gravy to simmer gently for 10 minutes, season to taste, and then strain into a warmed gravy boat or jug.

8 Garnish the lamb with rosemary sprigs and serve accompanied with roast potatoes and steamed quartered leeks.

## Cook's tip

• For a glossy finish, spread 2 tbsp honey over the lamb before the end of cooking.

| | |
|---|---|
| Preparation time | 20 minutes |
| Cooking time | 1 hour 50 minutes |
| Calories per portion | 550 Kcal |
| Fat per portion | 33g |
| of which saturated | 14.7g |
| Serves | 6 |

Saint George's Day

# Roast beef

To early Christians, the legendary slaying of a dragon by St George symbolised Christ's triumph over evil. But it was not until the 14th century that he was made patron saint of England, reputedly by Edward III on founding the Order of the Garter in St George's name.

**Fore-rib of beef** 2kg (4lb 8oz)
**Olive oil** 1 tbsp
**Salt and freshly ground black pepper**
**Plain flour** 125g (4½oz)
**Egg** 1 large
**Full cream milk** 300ml (½ pint)
**Butter** 15g (½oz)
**Full cream milk** 300ml (½ pint)
**Grated hot horseradish** 2-3 tsp
**Soured cream** 3 tbsp

### Cook's tip

● If you can't get hold of fresh horseradish, it is available in jars from a supermarket throughout the year.

| | |
|---|---|
| Preparation time | 30 minutes |
| Cooking time | 2 hours |
| Calories per portion | 683 Kcal |
| Fat per portion | 39g |
| of which saturated | 18g |
| Serves | 6 |

1 Preheat the oven 240°C/475°F/Gas 9. Wipe the beef well with kitchen paper and then smear it all over with the olive oil. Sprinkle the fat liberally with salt.

2 Place in a roasting tin, standing upright, and cook for 20 minutes. Then reduce the oven temperature to 180°C/350°F/Gas 4 and cook for 1 hour, basting frequently – this cooks the beef to medium-rare. For meat that is more well done, continue cooking until done to your liking – testing every 10–15 minutes.

3 Meanwhile, prepare the batter for the Yorkshire pudding. Sift 110g (4oz) of the flour and a good pinch of salt into a bowl and make a well in the centre. Break the egg into the centre and then gradually whisk it into the flour. As the mixture starts to thicken, gradually add the milk, whisking well until all the milk is incorporated and the batter is smooth. Cover and leave to stand.

4 Meanwhile, make the horseradish sauce. Melt the butter in a saucepan, stir in the remaining flour, add the milk and bring to the boil, stirring until the sauce thickens. Add the grated horseradish, season with salt and stir in the cream. Cover the surface closely with cling film, add the lid and keep warm.

5 When the beef is done to your liking, remove it from the tin onto a serving plate. Cover with foil and leave to stand until ready to carve. Increase oven temperature to 220°C/425°F/Gas 7.

6 Skim 3 tbsp of the fat from the roasting tin into a 12-hole patty tin (or a 19cm (7½in) round, ovenproof pie plate) and heat in the oven until sizzling hot. Stir the batter, pour it into the holes and cook for 15 minutes until the puddings are well risen and crispy.

7 To make the gravy, skim all but approximately 2–3 tbsp of the fat from the roasting tin into a small bowl and use for roasting potatoes. Stir 1–2 tbsp flour into the fat remaining in the tin (just enough to absorb the fat), and add the beef stock.

8 Place the roasting tin over a moderate heat and bring to the boil, stirring and scraping the browned residue from the bottom of the tin. Simmer for 5 minutes, season well and then strain into a warmed gravy boat. While the gravy is simmering, reheat the horseradish sauce and pour it into a serving jug or bowl.

## St Andrew's Day
# Roast saddle of venison

Andrew, the patron saint of Scotland, was one of the apostles. Some 300 years after his death, legend has it that a monk moved his bones to Scotland. The place he came ashore is now known as St Andrews. This dish combines traditional Scottish food and flavours.

**Venison** 3.2–3.6kg (7–8lb) prepared saddle, removed from refrigerator 2–3 hours before cooking, to bring to room temperature

**Butter** 150g (5oz), softened

**Juniper berries** 2 tsp, crushed

**Salt and freshly ground black pepper**

**Un-smoked, rindless streaky bacon rashers** 12

**Red dessert apples** 4 medium to large

**Unsalted butter** 40g (1½oz)

**Soft light brown sugar** 1 tbsp

**Lemon** 1, strained juice only

**Whisky** 4 tbsp

**Plain flour** 1 tbsp

**Red wine** 150ml (¼ pint)

**Chicken stock** 300–450ml (½–¾ pint)

**Redcurrant jelly** to garnish

1 Preheat the oven to 200°C/400°F/Gas 6. Wipe the saddle with kitchen paper to remove any blood and particles of bone. Blend the butter with the berries and smear over the top of the saddle.

2 Season the saddle well and cover the top with the bacon – weaving together like basketweave. Secure with thin string by sliding it under and along the ribcage on each side, and tying on top. Place the saddle in a roasting tin and cook for 20 minutes.

3 Reduce the oven temperature to 190°C/375°F/Gas 5. Remove the venison from the oven and loosely cover it with foil. Cook for 1–1¼ hours – or until done to you liking – basting frequently. Test by inserting the tip of a knife into the flesh – if the juice runs slightly red, it should be medium-done.

4 Meanwhile, cut each apple in half and remove the core. Place the butter, sugar, lemon juice and whisky in a lidded frying pan and heat until melted. Place the apples cut sides down in the pan and baste. Cover and cook for 15–20 minutes, turning halfway, and basting until the apples are softened. Keep warm.

5 Transfer the saddle from the roasting tin onto a large serving platter. Remove the string and loosely cover with the foil. Leave to stand in a warm place (not the oven) while making the gravy.

6 Skim off fat from the roasting juices until you have 2–3 tbsp left. Stir in the flour, add the red wine and bring to the boil, scraping the residue from the pan bottom, and adding the stock as the mixture thickens. Strain the sauce into a clean saucepan and bring to the boil. Reduce the heat and allow to simmer.

7 Remove the apples from the pan, brush with redcurrant jelly and arrange around the saddle. Strain the sauce into a jug and serve with sautéed potatoes and peeled roasted beetroot or red cabbage with chestnuts.

## Cook's tip

• Take care not to over-cook the venison, as the meat will become dry. Also remember that the meat will continue cooking in its own heat when removed from the oven, and while you make the gravy.

| | |
|---|---|
| Preparation time | 40 minutes |
| Cooking time | 1¼–1½ hours |
| Calories per portion | 513 Kcal |
| Fat per portion | 18g |
| of which saturated | 7.5g |
| Serves | 8 |

Halloween

# Toffee apples

Toffee apples are often associated with Halloween or Bonfire Night. To make them look more like fairground apples you can add some red food colouring to the toffee as it's boiling, but for a more natural look, keep it plain.

**Apples** 6–8 small, washed and dried
**Water** 125ml (4fl oz)
**Granulated sugar** 250g (9oz)
**Golden syrup** 2 tbsp
**White wine vinegar** 1 tbsp
**Butter** 25g (1oz)

1 Press a wooden stick into the stalk end of each apple.

2 Pour the water into a saucepan and add the granulated sugar, golden syrup and vinegar. Place the pan over a low heat and stir until the sugar dissolves. Wash down any crystals on the side of the pan using a damp pastry brush. Increase the heat and boil rapidly until the syrup reaches hard crack stage on a thermometer (147°C/290°F). Remove the pan from the heat and add the butter and swirl it around. Plunge the base of the pan briefly in cold water to prevent the syrup getting hotter.

3 Dip each apple in turn into the syrup, and leave the excess to drip off before placing on a sheet of baking parchment, with the sticks upright, to cool and for the toffee to set. If the toffee gets too set in the pan, it may be re-warmed gently over a low heat. If you want the toffee to be a thicker coating on the apples, they may be dipped a second time.

4 Wrap the apples in cellophane when they are cold to help prevent them from going sticky, otherwise if it's humid they will absorb moisture from the atmosphere and will go sticky quickly.

## Cook's tip

• If you don't have a sugar thermometer, then drop a little of the syrup from a spoon into a bowl of iced water and if you can press it into a ball with your fingers, then it's ready.

Preparation time – 5 minutes
Cooking time – 10 minutes
Calories per apple – 266 Kcal
Fat per apple – 4g
of which saturated – 2.2g
Makes – 6
Suitable for vegetarians

Christmas

# Honey-glazed ham

York ham, with an apricot compote glaze, was served to Queen Victoria every Christmas as she loved apricots. Scotts of York have been curers of Yorkshire hams and bacon for centuries. These days you can also buy smoked or unsmoked gammon.

**Gammon joint** 2kg (4lb) smoked or unsmoked
**Onion** 1
**Cloves** good handful
**Bay leaf**
**Peppercorns** 8
**Apricot halves in fruit juice** 410g can
**Light muscovado sugar** 5 tbsp

1 Rinse the gammon and put it in a large pan with the onion, studded with six cloves, the bay leaf and peppercorns. Add enough water just to cover the meat. Bring to the boil, cover the pan and simmer as gently as you can for 1 hour 50 minutes.

2 Drain the apricots, reserving 8–10 of the firmest, best-shaped ones. Mash the rest with the sugar for the glaze.

3 Preheat the oven to 190°C/375°F/Gas 5. Lift the gammon out of the pan (keep the stock for cooking the vegetables) and put into a roasting tin with the onion and about 300ml (½ pint) of the cooking water. Leave the meat for about 5 minutes until cool enough to handle, then remove the string and skin and score the fat into a diamond pattern. Stud the top with cloves, if you like, then spread the apricot mixture over the top, using your hands.

4 Roast in the oven, uncovered, for 40 minutes, until the glaze browns. Place the meat on a serving dish and garnish with the reserved apricots, warmed in the fruit juice. Make a sauce with the juices from the roasting tin. Serve hot with boiled potatoes and green vegetables or cold with bubble and squeak or salad, or in sandwiches.

## Cook's tips

• Do check whether the gammon you are buying needs soaking.
• If you don't want to roast the gammon, just carry on simmering it for another 30 minutes. Or you can leave out the simmering in a pan step and cook the gammon straight away in the oven at 180°C/350°F/Gas 4, loosely covered with foil for 2 hours 10 minutes. Remove the foil and the skin and put the glaze on, turn the oven temperature up and cook as in the main method.

| | |
|---|---|
| Preparation time | 15 minutes |
| Cooking time | 2 hours 30 minutes |
| Calories per portion | 379 Kcal |
| Fat per portion | 20g |
| of which saturated | 7.6g |
| Serves | 8 |

Christmas
# Traditional turkey roast

It was the Spanish who brought turkeys to Europe – after their invasion of Mexico in the 16th century. However, the English name reputedly derives from the fact that the bird was discovered in Turkey, and brought to England by our sea merchants.

**Bronze turkey** 6kg (12lb) oven-ready bird
**Butter** 25g (1 oz) softened

For the stock
**Giblets from turkey,** well washed
**Onion** 1 large, peeled and quartered
**Carrot** 1 large, peeled and sliced
**Parsley** 1 large sprig
**Bay leaves** 3
**Rosemary** 1 large sprig
**Black peppercorns** 1 tsp
**Chicken stock or water** 900ml (1½ pints)

For the stuffing
**Frozen peeled chestnuts** 225g (8oz)
**Chicken stock** 300ml (½ pint)
**Butter** 50g (2oz)
**Olive oil** 1 tbsp
**Smoked rindless streaky bacon rashers** 225g (8oz), cut into thin strips widthways
**Onion** 1 large, peeled and finely chopped
**Lean, good quality pork sausages** 400g (14oz), skinned
**Chopped parsley** 4 tbsp
**White breadcrumbs** 110g (4oz)
**Mixed dried herbs** 1 tbsp
**Lemon** 1, finely grated rind only
**Egg** 1 large, beaten
**Salt and freshly ground black pepper**

For the cranberry sauce
**Cranberries** 250g (9oz), washed, any stalks removed
**Orange** 1 large, finely pared rind and strained juice
**Caster sugar** 175g (6oz)
**Mixed ground spice** ½–1 tsp

For the gravy
**Roasting juices from turkey** see method
**White or red wine** 2–3 tbsp, optional
**Plain flour** 2–3 tbsp
**Chicken stock** 500ml (1 pint)

1 **On Christmas Eve,** prepare the stock. Place all the giblets except the liver in a saucepan and bring to the boil. Reduce the heat and skim off the scum that has risen to the surface. Add all the remaining ingredients, cover and cook gently for 1½ hours. Strain through a sieve, allow to cool, cover and refrigerate.

2 To make the stuffing, place the chestnuts in a saucepan, add the stock, partially cover and cook gently for 25 minutes, or until softened and most of the stock has been absorbed. Pour the nuts into a sieve placed over a bowl to drain, and leave until cold.

3 Meanwhile, chop the turkey liver and put into a large bowl. Heat the butter and oil in a frying pan, add the bacon and cook until browned and crispy. Add to the turkey liver.

4 Add the onion to the fat and cook gently until softened, then add to the liver and bacon and cool. Add the chestnuts and all the remaining ingredients, season well and mix together.

5 To make cranberry sauce, place all the ingredients in a stainless steel saucepan, partially cover and cook gently until the cranberries are softened and the juices are reduced by half. Transfer to a serving bowl, allow to cool, cover and refrigerate.

6 To prepare the turkey, wipe the inside clean with kitchen paper. Stuff the neck end only with the stuffing, but not too tightly. Make any excess stuffing into balls and cook separately.

7 Smooth the neck skin evenly over the stuffing and secure with fine skewers. Smear the turkey all over with the softened butter. Put onto a large plate, loosely cover with foil and refrigerate.

8 **On Christmas Day,** remove the turkey from the refrigerator early in the morning to allow it to come to room temperature. Preheat the oven to 220°C/425°F/Gas 7. Place a roasting trivet or wire rack in the roasting tin and put the prepared turkey on top.

9 Cooking times for turkeys will vary according to their size, and also their type. Generally, cook for 40 minutes, then reduce the oven temperature to 180°C/350°F/Gas 4 and continue cooking for 1½–2 hours, basting frequently until cooked. To test it's done, pierce the thigh at the thickest part – the juices should run clear yellow.

**10** Carefully remove it from the roasting tin onto a serving plate, loosely cover with foil and leave to stand. Cook the stuffing balls while preparing the gravy and attending to the vegetables.

**11** To make gravy, skim the fat from the roasting juices into a bowl, strain through a sieve and set aside. Pour the wine into the roasting tin, and bring to the boil, scraping the browned residue from the pan's bottom. Then strain into the bowl of juices.

**12** Pour 3–4 tbsp of the turkey fat into a saucepan and stir in the flour. Add the stock and strained juices and bring to the boil, stirring. Reduce the heat and allow to boil gently for 3–4 minutes, until reduced. Pour into a gravy boat for serving. Garnish the turkey with sprigs of rosemary and serve.

## Cook's tip

• Grilled chipolata sausages and bacon rolls are a delicious and traditional accompaniment for a roast turkey. Cook with the stuffing balls: 35–45 minutes.

Preparation time – 2 hours
Cooking time – 2 hours
Calories per portion – 1100 Kcal
Fat per portion – 50g
of which saturated – 19.2g
Serves – 8
Suitable for freezing

Christmas

# Kent plum pudding

This type of pudding is found in most regions around the country, just with a different name and a slight variation on the ingredients. This rich, fruity, nutty recipe is derived from the Sussex pudding. Not quite as rich as a traditional Christmas pudding, it can be made a few days before, then steamed for an hour before serving.

**Butter** 50g (2oz) plus a little extra

**Clear honey** 50g (2oz)

**Cooking apple** 1 small, peeled, cored and diced (110g/4oz prepared weight)

**Dried figs** 110g (4oz) 6 figs, stalks trimmed, diced

**Raisins** 110g (4oz)

**Sultanas** 50g (2oz)

**Currants** 50g (2oz)

**Mixed peel** 50g (2oz)

**Muscovado sugar** 50g (2oz)

**Blanched almonds** 100g pack, finely chopped

**Hazelnuts, Brazil or Macademia nuts** 25g (1oz), chopped

**Stale white breadcrumbs** 75g (3oz)

**Mixed spice** generous ½ tsp

**Lemon** ½, grated rind and juice

**Eggs** 2, beaten

**Rum** 1 tbsp

**Brandy** 3 tbsp

### Cook's tip

• This is one of those recipes where you can put in whatever fruit and nuts you have in your cupboard that need using up! One version had a total of 175g (6oz) nuts so you can add more, or use less if you're not so keen on nuts. The figs really are good in it, but feel free to change the ratios of the other fruits to suit your tastes.

| | |
|---|---|
| Preparation time | 30 minutes |
| Cooking time | 3 hours steaming plus 1 hour reheating time |
| Calories per portion | 385 Kcal |
| Fat per portion | 17g |
| of which saturated | 4.9g |
| Serves | 8 |
| Suitable for vegetarians | |

1 Butter a 900ml (1½ pint) pudding basin and have a pan with a steamer and tight-fitting lid ready.

2 Put the butter and honey in a small pan and warm through over a low heat until the butter melts. Set aside.

3 Mix the apple with the dried fruits, sugar, nuts, breadcrumbs, spice, lemon rind and juice.

4 Add the butter and honey mixture, eggs, rum and brandy and mix well. Spoon into the bowl and press the mixture down. Cover with a piece of bakewell or greaseproof paper and then foil, both containing a pleat to allow for expansion during steaming. Tie with string.

5 Put the basin in the steamer with boiling water underneath. Cover and steam for 3 hours, topping up with boiling water every so often. Let the pudding cool without the foil and paper.

6 Cover and keep chilled for a few days. Put fresh bakewell and foil on top and steam for 1 hour to reheat the pudding. Turn it out, decorate with a sprig of holly and flame with warmed brandy if you like. Serve with cream or custard.

New Year

# Anglesey cakes

It was customary for children in Anglesey to receive small cakes when they went 'first footing'. They sang a short verse to wish their neighbours a Happy New Year and the cakes would be a thankful gift. Although they are referred to as cakes (or, in Welsh, teisienau sir fon), they are much more like very short biscuits.

**Unsalted butter** 225g (8oz), softened
**Caster sugar** 110g (4oz)
**Self-raising flour** 350g (12oz)
**Salt** ½ tsp
**Raspberry jam** 6 tbsp
**Icing sugar** 1 tbsp

1 Preheat the oven to 180°C/375°F/Gas 4. Mix together the butter and sugar until creamy and smooth, and gradually work in the flour and salt.

2 Bring together to form a firm dough and turn on to a lightly floured surface. Roll out to a thickness of 6mm (¼in) and using a 5cm (2in) pastry cutter, cut out 24 rounds, re-roll the dough as necessary. Cut holes from the middle of 12 rounds using a smaller cutter or the upturned end of a large piping nozzle.

3 Arrange slightly spaced apart on baking sheets lined with baking parchment and bake for about 10 minutes until risen and golden. Allow to cool on the baking sheets and then transfer to a cooling rack. Sandwich the rounds together with jam and dust lightly with icing sugar just before serving.

## Cook's tips

• The cakes spread a little during cooking so don't place them too close on the baking sheets – allow approximately 2.5cm (1in) between each.
• For more festive shapes, use star or holly leaf cutters.
• Freeze unfilled. Allow the cakes to cool and then place in a freezer bag or freezer-proof container. Freeze for up to three months. Thaw at room temperature and fill and dust as above.

| | |
|---|---|
| Preparation time | 20 minutes |
| Cooking time | 10 minutes |
| Calories per cake | 295 Kcal |
| Fat per cake | 16g |
| of which saturated | 9.8g |
| Makes | 12 |
| Suitable for vegetarians | |
| Suitable for freezing | |

# Index

# Previous books

Dairy Cookbooks are widely recognised as some of the most reliable recipe books ever written. With over 30 million sold, almost every household will have used a Dairy Cookbook at some point. The first book; *The Dairy Book of Home Cookery* was published in 1968 and has been revised and reprinted several times due to its unprecedented popularity. In recent years, three new cookbooks have been published; *The New Dairy Cookbook*, the *Quick & Easy Dairy Cookbook* and the *Year Round Dairy Cookbook*.

*The Dairy Book of Home Cookery* (416 pages) was last published in 1992, and contains hundreds of recipes; from how to make the perfect cheese sauce to creating an impressive soufflé.

*The New Dairy Cookbook* (192 pages) was published in 2001 and features 150 delicious new recipes for all occasions.

The *Quick & Easy Dairy Cookbook* (192 pages) was published in 2003 and has 130 tasty recipes, which can be prepared in less than 30 minutes.

The *Year Round Dairy Cookbook* (192 pages), published in 2005, features 130 seasonal recipes to give the taste buds a treat throughout the whole year.

For pricing and ordering details please ring:

## 01536 762922

# Suppliers List

In some recipes we have mentioned a specific ingredient and supplier. Please find their details below.

**Scotland**
Mr Lindsay Grieve
29 High Street, Hadwick,
Scottish Border TD9 9BU
Tel: 01450 372109
Champion haggis supplier

Highland Fine Cheeses Ltd
Tain, Blarliath, Ross-Shire
IV19 1LZ
Tel: 01862 892034
Cheese supplier (Caboc)

**North East and Yorkshire**
The Ribblesdale Cheesemakers
Ashes Farm, Selside, Settle
BD24 0JB
Tel: 01729 860231
Cheese supplier (Ribblesdale)

Shepherd's Purse Cheese Ltd
Leachfield Grange, Newsham,
Thirsk YO7 4DJ
Tel: 01845 587220
www.shepherdspurse.co.uk
Cheese supplier (Yorkshire Blue)

**North West**
Godfrey C Williams & Son
9–11 The Square, Sandbach,
Cheshire CW11 1AP
Tel: 01270 762817
Cheese supplier (Bowland,
Cheddar and farmhouse pickle,
Cornish Yarg and Shropshire
Blue)

**Western England**
Belton Cheese Ltd
Belton Farm, Whitchurch,
Shropshire SY13 1JD
Tel 01948 662125
www.beltoncheese.co.uk
Cheese supplier (Sage Derby)

Staffordshire Organic Cheeses
Newhouse Farm, Acton,
Newcastle-under-Lyme,
Staffordshire ST5 4EE
www.deaville.demon.co.uk
Cheesemaker (Staffordshire
Organic) with farm shop

**Eastern England**
Hartington Cheese Shop
Hartington, Derbyshire
Tel: 01298 84935
www.hartingtoncheese.co.uk
Cheese supplier (Dovedale)

Wild Meat Company Ltd
Low Road, Sweffling,
Saxmundham, Suffolk IP17 2BU
Tel: 01728 663211
www.wildmeat.co.uk
Game supplier

**South East**
Kelly Turkey Farms Ltd
Springate Farm, Bickacre Road,
Danbury, Essex CM3 4EP
Tel: 01245 223581
www.kellyturkeys.com
High quality turkey supplier

Teddington Cheese
42 Station Road, Teddington
TW11 9AA
Tel 020 8977 6868
www.teddingtoncheese.co.uk
Cheese supplier (Laverbread,
Smoked Cilowen Organic,
Waterloo and Tornegus)

**Wales**
Llanboidy Cheesemakers
Cilowen Uchaf, Login, Whitland
SA34 0TJ
Tel: 01994 448303
www.llanboidycheese.co.uk
Cheesemaker (Llanboidy)